TEEN MASTERY MANUAL:

Cultivating Social Confidence and Essential Habits for a Radiant Future

~ 2 books in 1 ~

This volume includes:

Book 1. Critical Life Skills for Teens: A Fun and Easy Guide to Develop Good Habits, Build Confidence, Master the Skills and Knowledge You Need to Achieve Independence

Book 2. Social Anxiety Workbook for Teens: 10-Minute Activities and Tools to Reduce Stress, Conquer Fear, and Boost Social Confidence

CRITICAL LIFE SKILLS FOR TEENS:

A FUN AND EASY GUIDE TO DEVELOP GOOD HABITS, BUILD CONFIDENCE, MASTER THE SKILLS AND KNOWLEDGE YOU NEED TO ACHIEVE INDEPENDENCE

BLOOMING MINDS

Book 1

CONTENTS

FREE BONUS

SCAN TO GET OUR NEXT BOOK FOR FREE!

INTRODUCTION

"PARENTS RARELY LET GO OF THEIR CHILDREN, SO CHILDREN LET GO OF THEM. THEY MOVE ON. THEY MOVE AWAY. THE MOMENTS THAT USED TO DEFINE THEM – A MOTHER'S APPROVAL, A FATHER'S NOD – ARE COVERED BY MOMENTS OF THEIR OWN ACCOMPLISHMENTS."

— MITCH ALBOM

Who needs life skills, right? I mean, you've come this far without them ...

The truth is, you've been acquiring life skills your entire existence, and you're in an incredible place right now as a result. Your childhood is in the past, and you're already in charge of many adult-related responsibilities. You got this far because of your perseverance. And what an amazing gift that is.

As you progress through life, you may encounter situations where you require skills typically not taught in school. Trust me; I know—I learned them the hard way. I still remember the time I came home from grocery shopping with a whole chicken, only to realize that I didn't have the faintest idea what to do with it ... and it certainly wasn't what I needed for the pasta dish I'd been hoping to make!

What's more, the closer you get to leaving home, the scarier it all becomes, and it isn't just about practical skills. You're about to begin an amazing journey to discover yourself, and that's frightening for everyone.

As a former social worker, I've met many young people who were anxious about the challenges of transitioning into adulthood. A middle school student I worked with once said something that's always stuck with me: "I want to be a grown-up, but I don't want to grow up."

Think about that for a second. It's relatable, right? You're at a tricky stage of life where you're no longer considered a child, yet the thought of being an adult is overwhelming, and it's challenging to envision being fully prepared for it. You want to be viewed and treated as mature and responsible, and you long for the freedom of adulthood, but the idea of leaving home is daunting.

When you're younger, you don't pay much attention to what your parents or guardians do to keep things running smoothly, but as you get older, you become more aware that there's a lot going on behind the scenes, and at some point, you're going to be in charge backstage. Meanwhile, you're navigating the turbulent waters of adolescence and the changes in your body and hormones, running into relationship problems and exam stress as you go. Yep—I've been there too!

The best thing you can do now is put yourself ahead of the game and amass the skills you'll need to leap into adulthood with confidence, and you're in the right place to do that. By the time you've finished reading this book, you'll feel much more prepared for the journey ahead of you, and you'll have acquired the skills and knowledge that will not only help you in adulthood but will make your teenage years easier to navigate too. You're about to discover things that aren't included in your school textbooks and which most adults take years and many mistakes to figure out (my chicken disaster being a case in point!), and you'll find yourself firmly on the launchpad to adulthood and ready to enjoy the ride.

I've met so many teenagers struggling with their lack of knowledge about the things they'll need to navigate the adult world that I decided it was time for me to do something that could really help. And that's what led me to write this book. No matter how much they love their kids, parents sometimes get caught up in work, health issues, or whatever else is going on in their lives, and that can lead to them missing what's needed during this critical transition for their children. My goal is to help them and make sure you're as prepared as possible to thrive in any situation life throws your way.

The knowledge you'll gain from reading this book will equip you with improved social and life skills. I hope you'll be as excited as I am about your transition into adulthood. It's going to happen either way, but being prepared will make the process a whole lot smoother and a ton less stressful.

Everything you need to learn to prepare for adulthood is right here waiting for you.

So let's get started, shall we?

HOW TO USE THIS BOOK

The goal of this book is to be a resource you can refer to no matter what age you are. It's designed to be there by your side every step of the way to adulthood, and it's there for support when you get there too.

You may be a middle schooler, or you may be older, and that means that different parts of the book might be relevant at different times. If something isn't relevant to you yet (for example, if you're too young to drive), you can always come back to it later. And if you find something you already know, just move on—you'll soon come across something new.

Throughout the book, I'll guide you through the key areas you're going to need skills in as you gear up for adulthood. Here's what's waiting for you:

- Chapter One: Staying Healthy

- Chapter Two: Hygiene and Appearance

- Chapter Three: Relationships and Social Skills

- Chapter Four: Handling Your Emotions

- Chapter Five: Organizational Skills

- Chapter Six: Problem-Solving and Decision-Making

- Chapter Seven: Driving and Car Maintenance

- Chapter Eight: Household Maintenance and Cleaning

- Chapter Nine: Grocery Shopping and Cooking

- Chapter Ten: Money Management

- Chapter Eleven: Further Education and Employment

- Chapter Twelve: Personal Safety

Feel free to start wherever you want. Depending on your current skill level, you may not need to spend much time in a particular section. Remember, there's no shame in revisiting any skill that you haven't acquired yet, even if you're worried you should have mastered it at a younger age—in fact, that's key to being a successful adult.

A NOTE TO PARENTS

As your teen continues to navigate their way through adolescence, they must develop good life and social skills that will be useful to them for the rest of their life. I know you've already done a tremendous amount of work to teach them these skills, and I realize the journey isn't easy. Sometimes you might feel hopeless and discouraged. But I've got your back! In case you missed something along the way, let this book be your helper to fill in any gaps. It will certainly help your teen, but it can help you too. Your support is the most valuable resource they have—and the most important thing for you to do is enjoy this ride with them.

1
EVERYTHING YOU NEED TO KNOW ABOUT STAYING HEALTHY

"HEALTH IS A STATE OF COMPLETE HARMONY OF THE BODY, MIND, AND SPIRIT."

— B.K.S. IYENGAR

You've probably heard it a million times: "Eat your veggies, and don't eat too much junk food or candy."

It's on repeat, like the chorus to your favorite song. It's all solid advice, and when you're a kid, it's policed by your parents. As you get older, though, more of that responsibility falls on you. But do you understand why caring for your body is so important? Your overall well-being—physically and mentally—is essential for living your life to the fullest. Whether you want to go bungee jumping, party all night, or ace your exams, you need good health on your side. So what does that mean for you?

EATING WELL

Taking care of your body involves more than just the food you put into it, but eating well is crucial at every stage of life—including right now.

During your teenage years, your body is growing rapidly, and it's not just your height that's affected. Your body composition is changing, and you're going through cognitive and sexual development too. Did you know that 50% of your adult body weight is acquired between the ages of 10 and 19? That's crazy! And if you look at it that way, it's clear to see why being a teenager can feel so much like riding a roller coaster. Your brain, heart, and bones are all developing, and you need the right fuel to keep it all going. Good nutrition is vital for supporting healthy growth and providing the best nutrients to the body—both in terms of quantity and quality. Those trips to the waffle house are totally fine in moderation, but your body needs real fuel too.

Failing to take in enough calories or nutrients can lead to health complications such as delayed puberty, stunted growth, and, if you're a girl, irregular periods, and much as I don't want to scare you, I think it's important to be aware of them. An inadequate diet can also affect your mood, energy, and performance—both physically and mentally. That's going to make you feel sluggish and emotional, and it's easy not to realize what's happening. Then before you know it ... feeling miserable and tired all the time becomes normal. Eating well also reduces the risk of health conditions and diseases later in life, supporting growth into adulthood and establishing good habits.

With this idea as our foundation, let's delve deeper and look at exactly what your body needs and how you can make sure you're providing it.

Energy Use

Did you know that the energy your body uses comes from the food and drinks you consume? That energy is used throughout the day for thinking, moving, and growing, so it's important to get the balance right. That means taking in the right amount of calories for your body, which differs from person to person according to weight, height, age, sex, and activity levels.

The calories you need come from the macronutrients in the food you eat. These are fat, protein, and carbohydrates—and no matter what crazy diets you might have heard about, they're all equally important. The following table shows you the calorie estimations for different age groups, although this does change a little depending on how active you are. If you play sports or move around a lot, you might need more calories, while if you're not very active, you might need less.

Age	Male	Female
13	2,200	2,000
14	2,400	2.000
15	2,600	2.000
16-18	2,800	2.000
19-25	2,800	2.200

26-45	2,600	2.000
46-50	2,400	2.000
51-65	2,400	1,800
66+	2,200	1,800

Let me add that counting calories isn't the best way to approach this, and I'm merely providing these guidelines to give you an idea of what your body needs. Instead of worrying about the numbers, focus on eating three delicious and nutritious meals a day and snacking on healthy treats when you feel hungry. Count your blessings, count your money, count your friends. Count anything you like, but not your calories. We'll look at how to measure healthy portion sizes in just a moment so you can avoid doing that.

We're fed a lot of messages by society about the ideal body image. You've been getting those messages ever since you were a little kid, and I'm sorry to say they don't go away when you get older. As a result, many young people try to lose weight by drastically reducing their food intake and cutting out food groups or skipping meals. Please don't be one of these people. These approaches aren't healthy because they mean you lose out on essential nutrients that your body needs to stay healthy. If you're concerned about your weight, talk to a healthcare professional before you make any big changes. They'll be able to tell you whether or not you really do need to lose weight and guide you to the healthiest way to do so.

HEALTHY CHOICES

Healthy nutrition is like balancing an equation. American literary critic Barbara Johnson once said, "A balanced diet is a cookie in each hand." I couldn't stop laughing when I first read it, but jokes aside, that's a terrible idea because it's not just about how much you eat; what you eat matters too—and two cookies certainly don't cut it. Here's the lowdown:

- Fruit and vegetables should make up half your plate at every meal. If you're not a big fan, try to sneak up on yourself and drink your fruit in smoothies or hide salad in your sandwich.

- Whole grains are healthier than refined grains, so opt for whole wheat bread, oatmeal, and brown rice over white bread, white rice, and processed cereals. To meet your protein requirements, focus on lean meats like chicken, turkey, lamb, and rabbit, as well as eggs, seafood, nuts, and beans.

- Forget the bad rap that fat often gets—you need it for your growth and development and for healthy hair and skin. You'll find healthy fats in olives, avocados, nuts, seeds, and oily fish like salmon.

- Include dairy products in your diet, such as low-fat yogurts, cheeses, and milk.

The writer Mark Twain said, *"The only way to keep your health is to eat what you don't want, drink what you don't like, and do what you'd rather not."* In other words, you must know what to avoid or consume in moderation. Heavily processed foods that are high in trans fats or sugars should be limited—that includes things like candy, sodas, cookies, chips, ice cream, and fries. A small amount of sodium is necessary for good health; however, too much salt can lead to high blood pressure, so don't eat more than a teaspoon a day (and watch out for packaged foods—they often contain a lot!).

HEALTHY SERVINGS AND ATTITUDES

This is crucial when it comes to maintaining a healthy lifestyle. You might have heard the joke, *"I'm on a seafood diet—I see food, and I eat it."* Funny though it is, it's not a healthy approach to eating. Be mindful of the portions and types of food you eat, and if you're unsure, a simple trick is to use your hand as a guide. The hand measurement system is always the best to follow as your hands are proportionate to your body, and the size never changes. Your palm is about the size of a protein serving; your fist is about the size of a vegetable serving; your cupped-hand is about the size of a carbohydrates serving; and your thumb is about the size of a serving of healthy fat. Remember, your body needs a variety of nutrients from different food groups, so try to include them all in your meals.

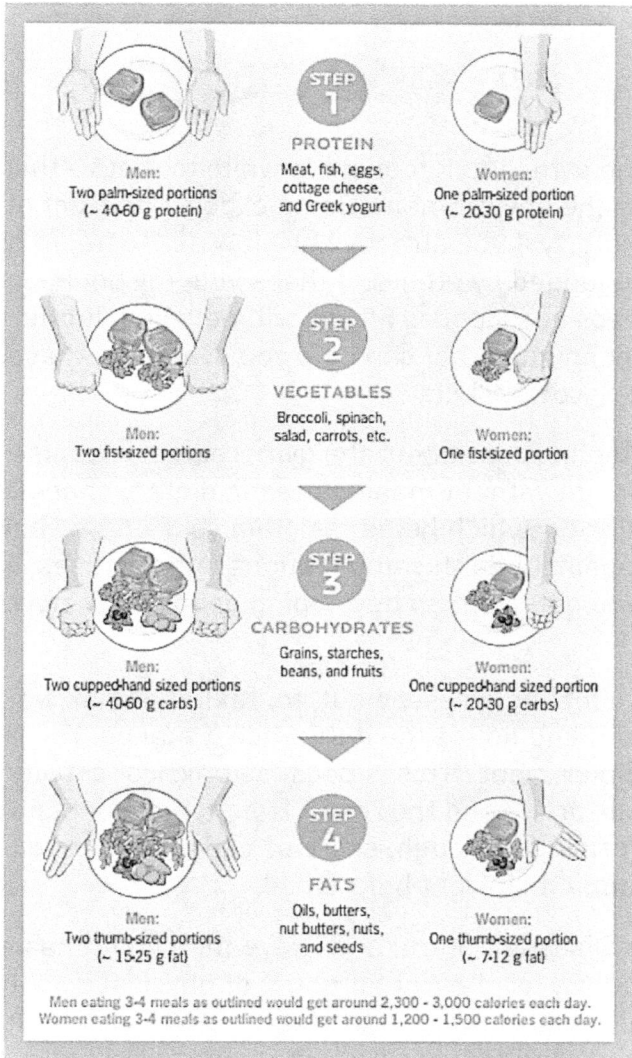

St Pierre Ms Rd, B. (2023). Infographic | The Best Calorie Control Guide. Precision Nutrition. https://www.precisionnutrition.com/calorie-control-guide-infographic

Your attitude towards food is just as important as what you eat. It's easy to fall into the trap of feeling guilty after eating certain foods or comparing yourself to others, especially with the pressure of social media and celebrity culture. Note that there's no such thing as a perfect diet or body. Everyone is unique, and that's what makes us so special. Instead of focusing on what you can't eat or what you don't like about your body, focus on what you can eat and what you love about yourself. Healthy eating and a positive attitude go hand in hand, and they both contribute to a happier, healthier you.

PHYSICAL EXERCISE

I used to hate the gym, and it took me a while to realize that what I actually disliked was the environment. Being exposed in front of others can be daunting, particularly if you already have low self-esteem or you're worried about being judged by others. If that's you, my book, *Social Anxiety Workbook for Teens by Blooming Minds*, will help you. It offers effective exercises and techniques that can help you overcome these challenges and enhance your social skills.

Whatever your feelings are about the gym, regular exercise will help you manage your weight without making drastic dietary changes. It allows your body to burn calories, which helps maintain your energy balance. It also helps arm you against health complications and diseases, which become more likely as you get older, so developing good habits now will make life easier later.

Next time you're feeling stressed out, try taking a brisk walk or dancing around your room and notice the difference it makes. You feel more relaxed and happier, right? This is because physical activity activates the chemicals in your brain, and the result is a mood boost and a reduction in stress. And surprisingly enough, exercise can also help you sleep better—as long as you don't do it right before bed.

The Centers for Disease Control and Prevention (CDC) has created a list of recommendations for the right amount of physical activity for different age groups, which you can see in the table below. I've included all age groups so you can see how your requirements will change as you progress through adulthood.

Age	Recommended Activity Level
3-5	Active play throughout the day
6-17	60 minutes of moderate to vigorous activity a day (Including bone strengthening, muscle strengthening, and cardio activities)
18-64	150 minutes a week of moderate activity plus muscle strengthening twice a week
65+	150 minutes a week of moderate activity plus muscle strengthening twice a week plus balance activities
Adults with dis-abilities or chronic conditions	150 minutes a week of moderate activity plus muscle strengthening twice a week (adapted to suit needs and abilities)
Pregnant women and women who have recently given birth	150 minutes a week of moderate activity

HOW TO GET YOUR EXERCISE

As you can see from the chart, right now, you should be getting about 60 minutes of exercise per day. Some of that can be moderate activity, but some of it should be of a vigorous intensity, which you should aim for around three days a week. Any activity that elevates your heart rate and makes you breathe harder counts towards this, so pick something you enjoy.

Here are some physical activities that you can consider besides going to the gym that can be practiced either in a class or at home:

- **Yoga:** This is an excellent option for improving your physical health while reducing stress and anxiety.

- **Dance:** This helps boost your self-confidence and improve your coordination, and you can do it at dance classes, parties, or even at home.

- **Martial Arts:** Martial arts, such as karate, taekwondo, or judo, can provide a structured and disciplined environment while teaching you self- defense skills and improving physical fitness.

- **Hiking or Nature Walks:** Being outdoors can significantly reduce stress and anxiety. Walking outside will improve your physical health and provide an opportunity for reflection and introspection—things you'll welcome when you're stressed out about school.

- **Swimming:** This will improve your cardiovascular health and muscle strength while providing a calming and relaxing experience.

- **Team Sports:** Taking up a team sport such as basketball, soccer, or volleyball is an excellent way to socialize and improve your physical fitness at the same time.

- **Cycling:** This is a great way to explore the outdoors while exercising. You can do it alone, or you can team up with your friends and family.

- **Rock Climbing:** This is a challenging and thrilling activity that can improve your strength and endurance while helping you build your self-confidence and overcome your fears.

- **Skateboarding:** A fun and creative way to exercise, this can be done alone or with friends. It will improve your balance and coordination while also providing an opportunity for self-expression.

Also include some muscle-strengthening activities. Lifting weights is good for this (and no, that doesn't mean you have to turn yourself into The Rock—anyone can lift weights, and it won't bulk you up). There are more subtle ways to get physical activity as well; tasks like cleaning your room, walking the dog, and taking out the trash will all help to keep you active.

The secret is to make exercise fun. If you hate gym class, that doesn't mean you hate exercise; it means that you've yet to find an activity you enjoy, and it may be one you're not even taught in school. Pro tip: exercising with friends is a beneficial strategy because it turns it into a social activity, enhancing the enjoyment factor and increasing your motivation.

SLEEP

AN IMPORTANT PART OF YOUR HEALTH

Sleep is essential not only for your physical health but also for your mental health, academic performance, and energy levels. Good sleep habits, especially during adolescence, can lead to improved physical health, proper growth and development, and a lower risk of illnesses.

WHAT HAPPENS WHEN YOU SLEEP?

When you first fall asleep, your heart rate and blood pressure drop. Your parasympathetic system takes control of your body, meaning your heart doesn't have to work as hard as it does when you're awake. In the moment you wake, as well as during the phase known as REM sleep, your sympathetic system activates again, and your blood pressure and heart rate go back to their normal waking levels. That's how you know you're not a vampire!

HOW YOUR SLEEPING PATTERNS AFFECT YOUR HORMONES, METABOLISM, AND IMMUNE SYSTEM

Sleep plays an important role in regulating hormones, metabolism, and immune system function. Hormones like progesterone, estrogen, and testosterone are produced during sleep and can impact your overall health. Disrupting your sleep patterns can also affect your metabolism, leading to a distorted sense of hunger and changes in how your body processes fat. In addition, getting enough sleep is important for immune system function, as a lack of sleep can leave you susceptible to colds and infections.

THE IMPORTANCE OF SLEEP FOR LEARNING AND MEMORY

The last piece of the sleep puzzle has to do with your capacity for learning and your ability to form long-term memories.

When you don't sleep enough, you may find you have problems with focus and clear thinking, resulting in a decline in academic performance and de-creased energy levels. It can also lead to a range of mental health issues in teens, such as depression, anxiety, and mood swings. Not only that, but poor sleep habits can leave you susceptible to developing sleep disorders, such as insomnia, sleep apnea, and narcolepsy, all of which can have long-term health implications.

Just as it has guidelines for physical activity, the CDC has published guide-lines for the recommended amount of sleep for different age groups. You'll find these in the chart below. Again, I've included the recommendations for all age groups so you can see how these changes throughout your life. It's crazy how much sleep babies need, right?

Age	Amout of sleep per day
4-12 months	12-16 hours
1-2 years	11-14 hours
3-5 years	10-13 hours
6-12 years	9-12 hours
13-18 years	8-10 hours
18-60 years	7+ hours

Getting into good sleeping practices now means they'll already be ingrained when you're older, when you may find—as many adults do—that sleep becomes more difficult.

ORAL HEALTH

Good oral health is crucial for your overall well-being. Bacteria in your mouth can cause respiratory and digestive diseases, so brush your teeth regularly—at least twice a day (ideally for two minutes), floss after each meal, and use mouthwash to remove any dislodged food particles. Keep your dental appointments just as seriously as your Netflix watch list. Besides preventing bad breath and tooth decay, having a clean and healthy mouth boosts your confidence and ensures a pleasant eating experience.

PRO TIPS:

- Avoid sugary snacks, and opt for fruits, veggies, and plain snacks.

- Chew sugar-free gum after meals to help stimulate saliva flow.

- Water is the best drink for your teeth, but if you must drink soda, use a straw to minimize damage. Don't brush your teeth immediately after consuming acidic drinks unless you want your teeth to erode faster than a sandcastle at high tide.

Cosmetic treatments like braces and tooth whitening can boost your confidence too, but it's beneficial to consider the pros and cons before deciding. Braces require extra care, and you'll need to avoid sticky or chewy foods. Tooth whitening may cause sensitivity and won't whiten fillings or crowns. It's not permanent and may affect your ability to eat certain foods comfortably. I know someone who had it done and nearly put herself off ice cream for life!

SURPRISING WAYS TO IMPROVE YOUR HEALTH

Healthy food, regular exercise, sufficient sleep, and good oral health are more obvious ways to keep your health in check, but there are a couple of less obvious ones too. One of those is having an active social life, which we'll talk about more later. Seeing your friends and family regularly will boost your mental health, and if you're also engaging in activities with them, you'll be improving your physical health too.

Another subtle health tip is to limit your use of technology. I know how tempting it is to reach for your devices and dive into the social media world, but spending too much time with your eyes on a screen can reduce your sleep quality, contribute to mental health problems like depression and anxiety, and increase the risk of developing problems with your attentiveness.

With your health in check, it's time to make sure you look the part. In the next chapter, we'll take a look at personal hygiene and grooming ... but not before a bit of motivation. You'll find one of these affirmations at the end of every chapter. Try saying it to yourself every day. Feel it. Believe it—you might be surprised at how powerful it is.

The only person I will compare myself to is the best version of myself.

2
STAYING CLEAN, SMELLING FRESH, AND LOOKING SHARP

A parent once told me about how her son used to hate taking baths when he was little. It was a constant battle, she said, and even as a young teenager, he needed reminding, or he would lie about whether he'd taken a shower. It was only when other kids started making comments about the way he smelled that he began to change his ways. His friends started ignoring him, and the bullying began. He learned his lesson the hard way, and the chances are, you already know that you don't want to smell like an old gym bag, and this isn't an issue you have. Nonetheless, personal hygiene is essential, and not everyone knows how to maintain it. Let's take a look at why it's important and what you can do to make sure you're on top of it.

PERSONAL HYGIENE BASICS

Keeping our bodies clean protects us from harmful germs that cause illness and disease while also preventing unpleasant body odor that could affect our social interactions. Just think of the poor kid from the beginning of the chapter.

Personal hygiene becomes even more critical during the teenage years as the body goes through changes that increase body odor. Developing good personal hygiene habits helps you to stay clean and comfortable in social situations.

HAND WASHING

You would think this is a common sense practice, but let's not forget about the outbreak of covid-19. Somehow we overlooked washing and sanitizing our hands regularly, and we all had to suffer. Your hands can spread germs to anywhere else on your body and other surfaces you've touched, which is why you were taught to wash them before and after eating, after playing with pets, after using the bathroom, etc., when you were little—it's one of the first life skills you ever learned. Remember to sanitize your hands and wash them thoroughly with warm water and soap every time you are near a lavatory, especially outside your home.

BATHING AND DEODORANT

The cause of body odor is a certain type of sweat gland called the **apocrine gland** in your armpits and around your genitals that develops during adolescence. The sweat from these glands doesn't evaporate as quickly as the sweat from the other type of sweat gland on your body (the **eccrine glands**), and the bacteria you naturally have on your skin reacts with it to cause body odor. Lovely thought, isn't it?!

How frequently you bathe is dictated by your body and the activities you do in daily life. How often you wash your hair will depend on your hair type (we'll discuss this later in the chapter), and you'll find the right routine for you through trial and error. Over time, you'll know how often your hair becomes greasy and find the right pattern for you.

For most people, applying deodorant once a day is a good fit. Deodorant is designed to mask underarm odor, while antiperspirants reduce sweat and keep you drier. Therefore, if you sweat a lot, you'll probably feel more comfortable using an antiperspirant deodorant. However, it's important not to overuse them because they can block your sweat glands, and that can lead to painful lumps. You can also reduce your body odor by minimizing the amount you sweat. You can do this by wearing loose, breathable clothing (cotton is a good fabric for this) and washing with antibacterial soap.

MenSTRUATIOn

Obviously, this section only applies to girls, so boys, feel free to move on. That said, it wouldn't do you any harm to know what girls have to go through every month, so stick with us for a moment if you can handle it!

We'll only scratch the surface here, so regardless of your age or experience so far, if you have more questions, remember that you can always discuss these with your family doctor or another woman in your family, be that your mom, your older sister, or a favorite aunt.

Perhaps you've heard about Premenstrual syndrome (PMS); it's when girls experience emotional and physical symptoms before or during their peri-od. Notice the changes in your body 7-14 days before your period starts. Symptoms may include mood swings, sadness, anxiety, bloating, and acne but typically subside after the first few days of your period.

Girls often experience cramps during the first few days of their period. To alleviate discomfort, some remedies you can try include placing a warm heating pad on your stomach and taking over-the-counter pain relievers such as ibuprofen (Advil, Motrin) or naproxen (Aleve). For more details about medicine, talk to your doctor.

Period tracking apps are good tools for preventing you from being caught unprepared, although it does take a while for some girls to hit a regular cycle, so it's not guaranteed. Always make sure you have feminine hygiene products with you whenever you're out of the house—even if you don't need one. You could end up being someone else's hero! Whether you use sanitary pads, tampons, or menstrual cups, keep something in your bag at all times in case of an emergency. If you have an irregular cycle, reusable period panties could be a good option for you, allowing you to stay clean and dry even if your period sneaks up on you and catches you unawares.

Practicing good menstrual hygiene helps to reduce odors and infections and makes you feel more comfortable.

MOST IMPORTANT STEPS:

- Before and after using your menstrual products, wash your hands thoroughly.

- Ensure your menstrual product is changed frequently (regardless of how heavy your flow is) to protect your genitals from bacteria and fungi that can breed if moisture becomes trapped.

- Wear breathable cotton underwear to keep you comfortable and healthy.

- Dispose of your products properly by wrapping them in tissue and throwing them in the trash to avoid plumbing blockages.

- If you use a menstrual cup, clean it daily and sanitize it once your period is over.

- Choose unscented sanitary products and toilet paper, as the scented variety can affect your natural pH balance and irritate your skin.

To wrap it up, make sure you drink plenty of water. This helps your health overall, but specifically, it will help prevent infections by flushing out your urinary tract.

GROOMING

I'm not going to separate this section by gender, so take which parts apply to you and leave the rest—you'll know which parts are relevant.

SHAVING FACIAL HAIR

The age at which you develop facial or body hair varies, so don't panic if you're not there yet. When you're ready, the first step is to decide whether you want to use an electric razor or a blade razor. I'd recommend an electric razor, as you're far less likely to cut yourself. The other bonus is that you won't need to use shaving cream that way. If you do decide to use a blade, however, you'll need to wet your face and then apply shaving cream before you start. If you don't, you'll end up with skin irritation and cuts.

HOW TO USE A RAZOR:

- Move the razor over your face in short, gentle strokes in the same direction the hair is growing in. (This will stop you from getting cuts while you're getting started, but once you're a dab hand, you can shave against the growth.)

- Rinse your razor between each stroke, and afterward, pat your skin dry with a clean towel.

- You may want to use aftershave or lotion afterward, but allow your skin to breathe a little first, as the skin is more sensitive. Look for alcohol-free aftershaves to minimize the burn. (You don't want to have the experience Kevin had in the movie Home Alone!)

- If you use a disposable razor, throw it away once you've used it four or five times, and never share a razor with anyone else—doing so puts you at risk of infection.

- If you decide to grow a mustache or beard, keep it neat and tidy by shaving and trimming it every day.

UNWANTED BODY HAIR REMOVAL

Many women like to shave their legs and underarms, but it isn't required: It's an aesthetic choice. If you do decide to do it, wait until there's enough growth there to make it worth while. Some girls are tempted to begin before there's been much change to the amount of hair they have, and this can cause irritation.

There are several options for removing hair. Let's take a look:

- **Shaving:** This involves removing the tip of the hair shaft with a razor and lasts one to three days.

- **Plucking/Epilating:** This involves using tweezers or a machine to pull out hair and lasts three to eight weeks.

- **Depilatories:** These are creams or liquids that remove hair from the skin's surface. The results last several days to two weeks.

- **Waxing:** This involves spreading sticky wax on the skin and quickly pulling it off, taking the hair root and dead skin cells with it. It lasts three to six weeks.

The most common way to remove unwanted hair is to use a disposable razor. If you do this, start by taking a shower or bath to soften your skin. Apply shaving cream, and shave in the direction of hair growth, going slowly and avoiding pressing too hard. Pay close attention when shaving around the knees and ankles, as these are the places you're most likely to get cut—pay close attention when you're working on them. This isn't the moment to daydream! Change your razor often, and use a clean cloth to apply pressure if you cut yourself. After drying off, apply moisturizer to prevent dry skin.

NAIL CARE

Taking care of your nails is important for staying healthy and looking good. Here are some tips for keeping your nails in tip-top shape:

- Trim them after a bath or shower when they're softer and easier to cut. Use nail clippers or scissors to cut your nails straight across, and round the corners a little to keep them strong. File rough edges with an emery board, but always file in one direction to avoid weakening your nails. Don't forget to sanitize your tools after each use.

- Don't bite your nails. This can damage the nail plate and make it more vulnerable to infection, as well as affect your teeth.

- Leave your cuticles alone, as they protect the nail root. If you have a hangnail, don't bite or tear it off. Instead, use nail clippers or scissors to cut it away carefully.

- To prevent problems with your toenails, make sure that your shoes have plenty of room for your toes to wiggle. Change your socks daily to avoid infections, and wear flip-flops in public places like locker rooms, showers, and pools to prevent athlete's foot, plantar warts, and other diseases.

- Finally, check your nails regularly for any signs of problems like dark streaks or nails that start to crumble or fall off. If you notice anything like this, see a dermatologist for help.

Manicure & Pedicure

It's totally normal to want to express yourself and explore your own style, but when it comes to nails, it's important to take extra care. Here's how you can do that:

- Keep your nails clean, dry, and preferably short to avoid infections.

- Avoid harsh nail polishes and removers with acetone, as this can dry out your nails and make them brittle. Use natural nail polish removers instead and add a base coat and a top coat. Color-wise, neutral tones are more appropriate to a school environment in most cases, but don't hesitate to explore your options.

- If you're taking care of your own manicure and pedicure, make sure to sterilize your nail care tools to avoid infections.

- Wash your hands thoroughly with soap, and moisturize them with a protective cream or organic oils.

- Be cautious when getting manicures or pedicures done at a salon: Ensure that the tools your nail technician uses are clean and sterile. Ask them to avoid touching your cuticles as they are very important for your nails' health, and consult a doctor if your nails regularly cause you pain.

Long nails, natural or artificial, with different shapes and designs are appealing, but it's important to be aware that germs can breed under your nails. If this happens, these can then be transferred to other areas of your body. This makes it essential to keep up with your nail hygiene—even when they look beautiful on the outside. You'll need to use a nail brush to scrub away the dirt and clip them regularly.

SKIN AND LIP CARE

If you have spots or pimples, rest assured that this is completely normal. It's because of the changes in your hormones and the excess oil produced by your skin at this age, combined with pollution and sweat. You may get attacked by breakouts anywhere on your body, but your face, shoulders, chest, and back are likely areas. You're most likely to be plagued by blackheads and whiteheads, but there are six types of spots you may encounter:

- **Blackheads:** These are small yellow or black bumps that develop when your pores are blocked.

- **Whiteheads:** These are firmer than blackheads and have a white top to them.

- **Papules:** These are tiny red bumps, and they're often sore.

- **Pustules:** These are similar to papules, but a build- up of pus causes them to form a white tip in the middle.

- **Nodules:** These can be quite painful. They're hard lumps that form under the skin's surface.

- **Cysts:** These are the most severe form of acne. They are large lumps filled with pus, and they can leave behind scars.

If you frequently have a lot of blackheads, whiteheads, or pimples in the same place, you may have acne. Acne is a common skin problem that the American Academy of Dermatology says affects 80-90% of teenagers. It occurs when your hair follicles get clogged with dead skin cells and oil. Taking care of your skin is, therefore, important—especially as you get older. Let's look at some easy steps to get you started.

Cleanse: Wash your face regularly to remove all the extra oil, dirt, and buildup that clogs your pores and causes pimples. Use warm water, and pat dry with a clean washcloth. Aim to wash your face twice a day, but try to at least do it after school—and if you play a sport, then it's super important to wash your face afterward.

Moisturize: Even if you have oily skin, using the right type of lotion or moisturizer for your skin type can help protect it and control oil production. Use an oil-free moisturizer with SPF 15 or higher to protect yourself from the sun's harmful rays.

Treat: Acne is common during your teenage years. Use a medicated wash with 1-2% salicylic acid or benzoyl peroxide to help clear up breakouts. Use these products on the whole acne-prone area, not just on individual pimples or spots.

Prevent Breakouts: Wash your hands frequently, and avoid touching your face; clean your phone regularly, change your pillowcase often, wash your face after workouts, and drink plenty of water. If things get more serious, schedule a visit to see your pediatrician, family doctor, or dermatologist.

If you're new to taking care of your skin, here are some simple ways to get started:

- Be consistent and patient, as it takes time to see results. Stick to your routine every day for at least a month.

- Keep your products in the same place, like on the sink counter or in the shower, to make it easier to stick to your routine.

- Put a note on your mirror with each step of your routine as a gentle reminder.

If you wear makeup, it's important to know a little more about your skin type too. There are four main types of skin, and each one needs to be treated differently.

- **Normal Skin:** This is smooth and even-toned, with few blemishes or red spots. Wash your face two to three times a day with a mild cleanser or plain soap and water.

- **Dry Skin:** This can be itchy, scaly, and rough, with almost invisible pores. Wash your face daily with a mild cleanser and moisturize with a fragrance and alcohol-free face cream. Avoid very hot showers, exfoliating, and excessive washing or scrubbing, which can increase dryness. Follow the same directions if your skin is sensitive.

- **Oily Skin:** This is acne-prone, with open pores, a shiny complexion, and blackheads. Wash your face three times a day with warm water and a cleanser that contains salicylic or lactic acid, as this will help to dissolve any dirt and impurities. Your moisturizer should be free of oils and have hydrating properties. Use cosmetics that are "non-comedogenic" to prevent clogging your pores.

- **Normal/Combination Skin:** This can be oily in the T-zone (forehead, nose, and chin) and dry elsewhere.

Wash your face two to three times a day with plain soap and water. Moisturize only the dry areas of your skin and use a hydrating mist spray for the entire surface of your face.

Unless your skin is dry or sensitive, keep your skin exfoliated using a clay-based exfoliant to reduce the risk of clogged pores and those dreaded spots. If you have a break out, try using a mask or a sulfur cleanser to dry your skin. You can also try facial washes and creams containing benzoyl peroxide, which is anti-inflammatory and antimicrobial. Never pop or squeeze pimples, as that can worsen acne. During the summer, use sunscreen—ideally with an SPF over 30—even if your moisturizer has added sunscreen.

Your lips need as much care as you give the rest of your face. Before you go to bed, try scrubbing them gently with a baby toothbrush smeared with a little moisturizing cream or lip scrub. Afterward, wash it off, and use a gentle lip balm to keep your lips smooth and crack-free. I like to make my own scrub using one teaspoon of both honey and sugar. This not only exfoliates and moisturizes the lips; it nourishes them too.

MAKEUP

> ## "MAKEUP SHOULD NEVER BE USED TO HIDE YOURSELF. IT SHOULD BE USED TO ENHANCE YOUR NATURAL BEAUTY."
>
> ## — KIRA CARL

The importance of having a good skincare routine and preparing your skin properly before applying foundation, concealer, and other cosmetic products cannot be ignored— it's your best friend for life. If you notice that wearing makeup causes your skin to break out, you'll need to pay close attention to whether certain products affect it and try changing to a different brand.

Keep in mind that, often, less is more. Instead of using a full coverage foundation on your entire face, use a concealer to hide only the blemishes. Use a loose powder to set it and get rid of the shine and extra oil. Blush those cheeks, and voila! You're good to go. Whether you prefer the minimalist look or you like to wear a lot of makeup, don't be tempted to leave your makeup on overnight. I've done this, and I can tell you exactly what happens—it clogs your pores, leads to breakouts, ruins your eyelashes, and ends with you cursing yourself. Use micellar water or another makeup remover to gently wipe it away before bed.

Keep your makeup bag clean and neat. Check the expiration date of your products, especially creams and liquids. If anything smells funny, throw it in the garbage, and change your mascara once every three months. Clean your brushes and sponges regularly to stop bacteria from building up, and when you're at home, keep your brushes on the countertop and not in a makeup bag. It's best to have two brush holders or cups, one each for clean dirty brushes. Avoid sharing brushes or makeup with other people, as this can spread infections like pink eye or acne.

HAIRCARE

Caring for your hair requires understanding it. If you have straight hair, you probably have the easiest job, but because the oil from your scalp can easily spread to the full length of your hair, it can look greasy and lifeless if you don't guard against this. If you have curly hair, however, you have the opposite problem—the oil from your scalp finds it harder to spread through the full length of your hair, and that can lead to dry ends. Here's what you'll need to do to look after each hair type:

- **Straight Hair:** Wash no more frequently than every two days using a sulfate-free shampoo. This will encourage your scalp to produce the right amount of oil. If you'd like a fuller look, opt for a conditioner with coconut oil in it, as this will hydrate each strand. To style it, you can use a volumizing mousse to make it appear thicker.

- **Curly Hair:** Wash twice a week using a hydrating shampoo and conditioner to reduce the risk of damage and dryness. Choose sulfate-free products to make sure your natural oils aren't stripped away. Reduce the risk of frizziness when you dry your hair by using a blow dryer with a diffuser and use a wide-toothed comb for detangling. To make your curls stand out, you can use a curl-defining serum after you wash your hair.

- **Wavy Hair:** This is a mixture of straight and curly hair, which means that if you're among us lucky people who have it, you probably suffer from both problems—the oiliness at the roots and the dryness at the tips. Wash your hair every 3-4 days, and dry it with a microfiber towel to avoid frizziness. Use conditioner after every wash, and moisturize the ends with a serum. For extra volume and reduced protein loss, try massaging your hair with coconut oil the night before you plan to wash it.

No matter what type of hair you have, there are a few tips that will help it look its best, the most important being to detangle it frequently (and gently!). It's also a good idea to have it trimmed every six weeks to keep the ends looking healthy. Boys, you may be tempted to go for whatever haircut is in fashion, but just because everyone else seems to have it, it doesn't mean it's the one best suited to the shape of your face. Ask your barber what would work for you and be guided by that. I guarantee it will look better than trying to rock the latest trend if it doesn't suit you.

Avoid products that contain silicones, phthalates, and sulfates if you can, as these are harsh on your hair. Try to minimize your use of heat-styling tools, but if you do use them, use a heat-protecting spray or serum to protect your hair from heat damage.

Finally—as if you needed another reason to eat healthily— make sure you eat plenty of vegetables and drink a lot of water! You'll be amazed by how much difference this will make to your hair.

DRESS SENSE AND CLOTHING SKILLS

You only need to think about Hagrid's suit for the trial in *Harry Potter and the Prisoner of Azkaban* to see that dressing well takes skill—unfortunately, not one that he has!

The starting point for acquiring this skill is picking the right-sized clothes. Anything too small or too big will instantly distract from the impression you're trying to create. If you're not sure what size you are, or you find it varies from store to store, try on several sizes of the same item to make sure you find the best fit for your body. If you're self-conscious about your appearance, it can be tempting to hide in oversized clothes, but this will have the opposite effect to the one you're going for.

What Hagrid had right was that he chose the appropriate clothes for the occasion. He was going to a formal event, so he picked a suit. I've got some super important advice to get you ready to slay any event that comes your way. Knowing how to dress for any occasion is a major key to success in life. Not only should you look good, but you should also arrive in the proper attire. So let's break it down.

First, you've got to check the weather and figure out what activities you'll be doing so you can make sure you'll be comfortable. Next, consider the vibe of the event—no one wants to be caught wearing bright colors at a funeral when everyone else is wearing black. Finally, whether it's formal or informal will determine what kind of outfit you should put together. Feel free to wear your everyday clothes at a casual gathering, but for a job interview, you must dress to impress. From head to toe, you need to look sharp and professional.

Remember, it's not just about choosing the right outfit, but also how you treat your clothes. Let me tell you, showing up in a wrinkled suit and sneakers to a job interview will NOT make a good impression. It tells the employer that you don't take pride in your appearance, don't understand professionalism, and don't take care of your things. Yikes! The moral of the story? Make sure your clothing is in excellent condition. Trust me; it'll help you land that dream job!

We're going to move away from looking after your body now and take a look at how you interact with the world around you—starting with your relationships. But before we do, it's time for that all-important affirmation. Say this to yourself as often as possible because it's true, and the more you believe it, the more confident and empowered you'll feel.

I am a unique person, and my presence is a gift to the world.

3
THE SECRET TO INTERPERSONAL SKILLS

"THE MOST BASIC OF ALL HUMAN NEEDS IS THE NEED TO UNDERSTAND AND BE UNDERSTOOD."

— RALPH NICHOLS

Have you ever asked yourself what interpersonal skills are? Understanding and being understood in return is a fundamental part of a healthy and helpful relationship, and when we strive to see another person's perspective, it becomes easier to avoid conflict.

In this chapter, we're going to look at social skills, manners, communication, and relationships—all of which will help you find these conflict-free interactions and navigate social situations with ease. If social situations make you feel anxious, having these skills under your belt will make them a little easier, but if you're looking for extra fortification, try my other book, Social Anxiety Workbook for Teens: 10-Minute Activities and Tools to Reduce Stress, Conquer Fear, and Boost Social Confidence. That one's specifically designed to help you build your confidence in social situations, and when you do that, the social skills we'll look at in this chapter will really come into their own.

COMING TO GRIPS WITH SOCIAL SKILLS

We talk to people every day, and it might not seem like there's much skill involved, but social skills are crucial to every part of life—everything from your future relationships to your career success depends on being able to interact well with others. Let's take a look at exactly what's involved.

EYE CONTACT

Eye contact shows the other person that you're paying attention and that you're interested in what they're saying. It also helps to focus the conversation and allows you to read the other person's facial expressions, which leads to better understanding.

This is one of the most important parts of the social skills equation, but many teenagers feel uncomfortable with it. If you're one of them, and making eye contact makes you want to run for the hills, here are a few tips to help you out:

- Try the 50/70 rule: Hold eye contact about 50% of the time you're talking and about 70% of the time you're listening.

- Try holding eye contact for 5-10 seconds; then, allow yourself to look away for a moment before going back to it.

- When it's time to look away, do so slowly so that you don't seem nervous.

TALKING TO ADULTS AND USING NAMES

Casual greetings are fine with your friends, but "Hey bruh" or "Hey dude" isn't going to cut it if you're talking to a teacher, a prospective employer, or even your parents. In these situations, using the person's name is the appropriate way to address them, and you'll need to do that when you're introducing them to someone else. Making an effort to remember and use someone's name not only makes a good impression; it makes that person feel valued, and that goes a long way towards building positive relationships. Remember that it isn't always appropriate to use someone's first name either—if your teacher is called John Smith, the correct way to address him is by Mr. Smith. Mary Jones will be Mrs. Jones or Miss Jones, depending on whether or not she's married.

There are, of course, times when you don't know someone's name. When you're talking to an adult in this situation, whether it's a sales assistant or the mailman, it's appropriate to use honorifics (these are words that show respect). For men, this is sir; for women, this is ma'am—and it applies to all adults, regardless of their age. For example, you might say, "Excuse me, sir," when you want to ask a salesperson for help, or "Thank you, ma'am or madam," when a lady gives you directions.

You may not have had much experience with talking to adults beyond those in your family and at school yet, and that might make you feel a bit insecure. I promise you it gets easier with practice. Try to put yourself in

CRITICAL LIFE SKILLS FOR TEENS

more situations where you have to talk to adults—whether that's teachers around the school who you don't normally work with, your best friend's mom, or a random old lady waiting for the bus.

Reciprocal Conversation

One of the secrets to a natural, easy conversation is to meet one question with another. If that random old lady at the bus stop asks, "How are you?" you can keep the conversation moving by asking her the same question. If your hairdresser asks you if you're going on vacation over the holidays, you can answer and then ask her what her plans are. This is known as reciprocal conversation, and it shows that you're just as interested in the other person as they are in you. It also makes you feel a ton less awkward because it avoids those uncomfortable silences. To really level up, try to be the first one to ask the question.

Understanding Body Language

Some studies say that about 60% of what we communicate comes from nonverbal language. I talk a lot about this in my other book, Social Anxiety Workbook for Teens, so we'll just lightly touch on it here, and you can always visit the workbook for more information.

Body language and facial expressions are crucial aspects of nonverbal communication, which conveys emotions, thoughts, and attitudes. Facial expressions are highly expressive and often indicate happiness, confusion, or frustration, while body posture can show confidence, dominance, or submission. Hand gestures can also express meaning, and tone of voice can share emotions such as anger, sadness, or excitement. Paying attention to these nonverbal cues is essential for better understanding the meaning and intention behind a message, leading to stronger connections and relationships. When you recognize these subtle signs, it helps you know how to approach the interaction.

INTRODUCING PEOPLE

Casual introductions are fine when you're just introducing friends to each other, but as you get older, you'll find more of a need for formal introductions. The trick with these is talking to the person you want to honor first. For example, if you're introducing your friend to your grandma, you might say, "Grandma, this is my friend, Amber." You'd then turn to Amber and say, "Amber, this is my grandma, Helen." Formal introductions like this should generally be made when you're introducing someone to an adult. For bonus points, make sure you make eye contact when you do it, and gesture to the person you're introducing with your hands.

GOOD LISTENING

"Most people do not listen with the intent to understand; they listen with the intent to reply." (Stephen R. Covey) This is exactly what we want to avoid. Listening is more than just waiting for your turn to speak. It's about truly understanding others and holding back opinions until it's the right time to share them. Show you're listening with nods and acknowledgment at the appropriate moment.

SHOWING EMPATHY

Expressing empathy shows other people that we care and want to support them. Here are a few ways you can do it:

- **Put yourself in their shoes**. Consider what the other person might be experiencing in their life. Understanding their perspective helps you connect and empathize with their emotions.

- **Show you care.** If someone's telling you about their problems, it's because they need your support. Ask them how they're feeling, and see if there's anything you can do to help.

- **Acknowledge their feelings.** When someone tells you that they feel annoyed about something, for example, you can acknowledge their feelings by asking them what happened. If you brush off how they feel, they won't feel respected, and they may stop sharing their feelings with you, and this will harm your relationship.

- **Ask questions.** When we're trying to develop empathy, it's important to ask meaningful questions to encourage the other person to share more about how they feel. If, for example, your friend has just told you that she broke up with her boyfriend, you might ask her what happened to help her open up. This will show that you care and are holding a safe space for her to share her feelings.

- **Mirror the other person's responses.** If someone writes you five paragraphs in a message and you respond with one line, the conversation will break down pretty quickly. They're being open, and you're indicating that you're closed off. When you mirror their signals, however, you build rapport with them. For example, if your friend tells you something personal, you can reciprocate by sharing something personal and relevant about yourself in return. This doesn't mean you should copy everything they say or do, but responding in kind will put you in the same zone.

- **Don't jump ahead in the conversation.** If someone tells you they failed their test, it's a mistake to jump straight to the end of the conversation and say, "I hope you pass next time." A more empathetic way to respond is to ask how they're feeling and help them move forward by asking questions. You might ask what went wrong or what they plan to do next, for example.

- **Don't judge.** When you pass judgment on someone, you shut down the conversation, and the other person will close off. Listen to what they have to say, and try to avoid making assumptions.

- **Show your support.** Encourage the other person, and let them know that you have their back. Not everyone is looking for you to solve their problems— they just want you to listen and show you care.

MAKING A GOOD FIRST IMPRESSION

It takes just three seconds for someone to form an opinion of you. One glance will take in your body language, appearance, mannerisms, and behavior. Present yourself wrong, and you could end up creating a false impression of yourself—and it may not be favorable. You can avoid this by dressing appropriately for the situation (as we discussed in Chapter Two), arriving on time, smiling, being polite, listening attentively, and being genuine.

WAYS TO IMPROVE YOUR SOCIAL SKILLS

If you hang out with the same group of friends all the time, you're in your comfort zone. To sharpen your social skills, it's a good idea to put yourself in a range of social situations that require different things from you. Meeting new people is important too. Here are a few things you could try out:

- **Drama:** This is a great way for you to meet new people and challenge yourself to try something new. Research your local theater groups and see if they offer something for your age group. If you're not a big fan of being in the spotlight, you could always consider working in the production or costume department. You'll still meet lots of new people that way, and you'll gain some new skills too.

- **Activity Camps:** Summer camps offer a huge range of activities, and they're a great opportunity to make new friends. Every new activity you try, whether it's sport, music, drama, or dance, will be an opportunity to meet new people, and the activities will give you a focus, which will make it less intimidating.

- **Volunteering**: There are so many opportunities here. You could volunteer at a children's center or retirement home; you could work on a community arts or gardening project; you could offer your services at a homeless shelter or soup kitchen. Whatever you do, you'll find a great opportunity to sharpen your social skills at the same time as helping others.

- **Playing Sports:** Sports offer us a surprising amount of benefits in addition to being entertaining and keeping us fit. By joining a sports team, you'll get to work on your organization, teamwork, motivation, and leadership skills.

- **Classes:** If you have a particular interest or skill you'd like to develop, look for an evening class at your local school or community college. Whether it's an art class, learning a new language, or picking up a new skill like pottery or cooking, you'll get the added benefit of interacting with other students and your instructor. This will help you with your social skills—and you'll get to work on your creative expression too.

- **Live Events:** This may seem like an unusual one, but when you go to a live event with your friends or family, you become part of a collective experience. Dance shows, concerts, sports events, and quiz shows all put you in a large crowd with a lot of strangers. You'll get to enjoy the event with your friends, but you'll be exposing yourself to new social situations at the same time.

COMMUNICATION SKILLS

Good communication is essential for establishing and maintaining healthy relationships, whether it's with family, friends, colleagues, or romantic partners. It helps you to express thoughts, feelings, and needs, resolve conflicts effectively, and foster trust and understanding. Healthy communication isn't about you getting what you want, Violet Beauregarde-style: It's about you and the other person supporting each other and determining the best outcome for both of you.

THE FOUR STYLES OF COMMUNICATION

Did you know that there are four different styles of communication? Take a look and think about what best reflects you:

- **Passive:** You tend to keep your feelings, needs, and wants hidden to avoid conflict. You don't like making other people angry, and you often find yourself saying you don't mind when really you do.

- **Aggressive:** You often speak your mind without considering how the other person might feel. You consider your own needs, feelings, and wants first, and sometimes you shout or swear to communicate your point. People might describe you as being outspoken.

- **Passive Aggressive:** You use techniques like sarcasm, bullying, and giving people the silent treatment to express your feelings instead of speaking openly about what's on your mind.

- **Assertive:** You communicate honestly and are able to ask for what you need while still respecting other people's feelings and boundaries. This is the most effective style of communication.

Let's go over an example of these styles in context. How would you react in this situation?

Scenario: A friend asks if he can borrow your car. This will be a big inconvenience for you. How do you respond?

Passive: "Well, sure, I guess … ok. Do you need a full tank?"

Aggressive: "Have you lost your mind? No way! Why would I lend you my car?"

Passive aggressive: "Yeah right! It's not like I need my car to get to school or anything."

Assertive: "I need my car today, but I'm happy to give you a ride."

The ideal communication style to aim for is assertiveness, and by utilizing the skills you're acquiring in this chapter, you're on your way to becoming more confident, even if it doesn't come naturally to you at first. Just keep practicing.

Becoming an Effective Communicator:
Conflict Resolution Through Effective Communication

To move yourself closer to a healthy style of communication, try these tips:

- **Shift your focus to the issue, not the individual involved.** You may be tempted to assign blame to others, such as an unfair teacher, a self-ish sibling, or a backstabbing friend. However, it's important to avoid attacking the person and instead concentrate on the problem. In most cases, conflict arises due to different perspectives or needs that don't align.

- **Talk less, listen more, and take turns**. Make sure you really listen and understand the person who's talking rather than thinking about what you're going to say next. Be respectful, and don't interrupt the individual you're conversing with. When your turn comes, ask meaningful questions and express your opinion.

- **Understand your audience.** Be mindful of who you're talking to, and use that to inform how you speak. If you're talking to your teacher, leave aside the casual slang you'd use with your friends. Avoid using acronyms that others may not understand when communicating in text, like "TTYL," which might be okay with your friends but is inappropriate for a teacher or other adult. Be mindful of using appropriate language when communicating with different people in different contexts, such as emails to teachers or texting your grandmother.

- **Take notes.** If you're in a situation where you need to take in a lot of information, don't rely on your memory. If the family you babysit for has a list of jobs they'd like you to do, take notes while they're explaining them so that you don't forget anything. Don't hit "send" without checking. Whenever you're communicating in text, read over your message before you hit "send." Does it make sense? Are the spelling and grammar correct? Are you communicating clearly? Ask yourself how you would react if you got that message, and if it seems too emotional, step aside for a moment and come back to it later. Could your message create a conflict or solve a conflict?

- **Should this be a message or a call?** Ask yourself this question before you decide how you're going to communicate. If you have a lot to say, an Instagram message might not be the best medium, and a phone call might be better. Verbal communication allows for a two-way exchange and means things are less likely to get misinterpreted.

- **Get to the point.** Make sure your message, whether it's verbal or written, is clear by getting straight to the point. Say enough for the other person to grasp what you're trying to tell them, but don't clutter it with extraneous information. Bottom line? Don't ramble.

- **Be positive.** Even if you're speaking on the phone, try to smile—the other person will hear the positivity in your voice. When you show a positive attitude, you're more likely to get a positive response back.

- **Use "I" statements to resolve conflict.** When you say things like, "I feel uneasy when you do this," rather than, "You make me feel uneasy," you avoid blaming the person you're talking to, and this will make it much easier for you to resolve the conflict.

- **Be direct.** Aim to express your thoughts, feelings, and needs. If you don't communicate these things, you can't expect the other person to know them. Evaluate your assertiveness using the three C's of conflict resolution: remaining in a zone where you appear calm, confident, and compassionate.

- **Avoid raising your voice.** If you're having an argument, try to avoid yelling. This will only escalate the situation. The best thing to do if you feel yourself getting angry or upset is to step away from the conversation and cool off for a moment.

- **Be prepared to apologize.** Apologizing is a skill that many people find difficult to master. However, a sincere apology can work wonders when it comes to resolving conflicts. Parents who lead by example and apologize when they make mistakes help teach their teenagers to do the same. A good apology involves sincerity and does not include "buts" or excuses. The most effective apologies are those that acknowledge wrongdoing and express regret, such as saying, "I was wrong, and I'm sorry I hurt you." If you've had an argument, take responsibility for your part in it, and apologize. Sometimes apologizing first may diminish a conflict.

- **Look for compromises.** This doesn't mean you have to cave in if you disagree with something, but rather than insisting that your way is right, look for solutions that will work for both of you.

Using these tips will help you improve your communication style. Take what you've learned, and start applying the knowledge in your daily life.

MANNERS

When we show good manners, we demonstrate to other people that we respect them and consider their feelings. One of my favorite things about practicing good manners in everyday life is the little rewards you get for it. Hold a door open for a stranger or let them jump in the line in front of you, and you'll get a smile or a "thank you." Good manners make everyone feel good, and they serve to maintain harmony in every relationship we have.

Here's what you should be doing on a regular basis:

- Remember to say "please" and "thank you." Apologize when you've made a mistake or done something wrong.

- Ask for permission before acting.

- Don't answer your phone if you're in the middle of a conversation.

- Make eye contact when you're talking.

- Say "excuse me" if you bump into somebody or you need to interrupt them.

- Shake someone's hand when you meet them for the first time.

- Cover your mouth when you cough, sneeze, or yawn. Use good table manners.

- Answer when you're asked a question. Use appropriate language.

- Take turns in conversation.

DIFFERENT TYPES OF RELATIONSHIP

Throughout your life, you'll have several different types of relationships. These fall into four categories: family relationships, friendships, acquaintances, and romantic relationships. Let's take a closer look.

FAMILY RELATIONSHIP

Family relationships are the first ones we form in life with parents, siblings, and other relatives. These bonds can last a lifetime. Conflict with parents is normal in adolescence as you strive for independence, but remember, they're also trying to keep you safe. Hang in there!

FRIENDSHIP

Your friends are people you care about, trust, and have fun with. It's a two-way street—a reciprocal relationship—which means you both have to see each other as friends for it to work. You can have lots of friends or just a few, and some friendships may be deeper and more meaningful than others.

ACQUAINTANCES

Those people you're acquainted with but couldn't really call your friends also have a relationship with you. These are people you might bump into a lot—perhaps it's a friendly neighbor or someone you go to school with. It's important to be polite, but you might not share your secrets with them. Over time, some of those acquaintances could become friends, and then the dynamics of your relationship will change.

ROMANTIC RELATIONSHIPS

Romantic relationships form when you feel emotionally and physically drawn to someone who feels the same way about you. You spend a lot of time together, and sometimes, you may end up living together. You share a special bond that you don't feel with anyone else. Some relationships last for many years, while others may be shorter.

UNDERSTANDING HEALTHY RELATIONSHIPS

Whether it's your BFF, your crush, or your annoying little brother, there are certain qualities that make a good relationship. First off, it's all about mutual respect. That means you respect each other's boundaries and like each other for who you are (quirks and all!). No dissing or insulting allowed! Plus, you've got to value each other's thoughts, opinions, and time. And here's the secret sauce: trust, communication, and laughter. Sprinkle a healthy dose of that in, and you've got an awesome recipe for a healthy relationship. Voila! Now go ace that relationship game using the ingredients below!

- **Trust:** You both know that you can rely on each other for support, you believe what each other says, and you feel safe enough to share your secrets. You know that neither of you will intentionally hurt the other.

- **Honesty:** You can express your thoughts and feelings openly, discussing your needs, desires, and hopes without worrying about how each other will respond. Neither of you feels that the other person is keeping things hidden from them.

- **Growth:** You want the other person to enjoy the things they love doing, spend time with the people who are important to them, and learn new things— even when those things change.

- **Empathy and Communication:** You both seek to understand each other's points of view. You feel safe enough to share your feelings, and you feel heard when you do.

- **Balance of Power:** You both feel like you're equal. You can each make decisions for yourself without worrying about being judged, and you respect each other's independence and beliefs. Neither one of you will pressure the other to do something they're uncomfortable with, and both of you work equally hard on maintaining your relationship.

- **Compromise and Problem-Solving:** No matter what type of relationship it is, conflict is bound to come up every now and then. In a healthy relationship, you can work together to solve the problem and compromise to find a solution that suits you both.

- **Individuality:** You don't have to compromise who you are when you're together, and neither of your identities relies on the other. It's ok to have other friends, and it's ok if those relationships look very different.

There's such a thing as an unhealthy relationship, too. And while it's obviously not something you want to aspire to, it's worth being aware of what one looks like so you can take steps to correct it if it starts to form. Here are some signs of an unhealthy relationship:

- **Control:** One person tells the other one what to do and makes all the decisions. They may get jealous or try to separate you from other people in your life.

- **Hostility:** One person picks fights or tries to antagonize the other, which may lead to that person changing their behavior in order to avoid conflict.

- **Dishonesty**: You lie or withhold information from each other.

- **Disrespect:** One person makes fun of the other for their interests or opinions, or they don't respect their boundaries or property.

- **Violence:** One person uses force or aggression in order to get their way.

BUILDING EFFECTIVE RELATIONSHIPS

Let me tell you a story.

Judy's closest friend had just moved away with her parents. She was exhausted, and she felt the sadness deep in her stomach. Her brain responded by giving her a stream of negative thoughts: "I'll never be able to cope ... I'll have no one to talk to at school... I'll always be alone ..." As she focused more and more on the idea that everything was collapsing and she would be alone for the rest of her life, she grew distant from her family.

It took time, but slowly, Judy began to accept the change and started to build other friendships. She kept in touch with her friend, but she moved on with her life and started to open up again.

There will be many times in your life that you get so comfortable with the people surrounding you that when something changes, you will feel unsettled, maybe even freak out a bit. That's a perfectly normal reaction, but even when things don't go our way, we must adapt and open ourselves up to new relationships. So how can you do that?

The first thing I'd suggest is making sure you have a variety of relationships. As you form relationships with friends, other students, family members, teachers, colleagues, and instructors, you expose yourself to more varieties of relationships, which will inform every new one you have in the future.

It's also helpful to reflect on your relationships and consider what works for you and what doesn't. Try this exercise:

1. Make a list of people you enjoy spending time with. Consider how they make you feel and what you like about being with them. Think about their qualities. Perhaps they're a supportive and non-judgemental parent, a funny and honest friend, or a kind and helpful teacher.

2. Now write a list of the people in your life who you don't make an effort to spend time with—maybe they're classmates or colleagues. Consider the reasons you don't choose to spend time with them.

3. Make a new list of the people who you don't enjoy spending time with. Why is that? Is it that they're always negative or they don't pull their weight? Is it because they make fun of you or you can't trust them with your secrets? How do they make you feel?

4. Think about the three categories, and consider whether there are any themes coming through. Can you see signs of bad relationships and signs of good ones?

Having a good understanding of which relationships are the most important helps you prioritize them and seek the most nourishing relationships going forward. So, how do you attract more of those relationships?

The answer's surprisingly simple: It starts with recognizing that the people around you influence you. Surround yourself with those who inspire and support you while challenging you to grow. Mirror the positive traits you want to see in others to attract similar qualities in your life. Focus on the positive, and avoid attracting negative traits.

You may have noticed that we haven't touched much on emotions in this chapter, even though they're highly influenced by your relationships. That's because they get a chapter all of their own, which is coming up next—right after another affirmation you can use to build your confidence and remind yourself how important you are.

No one can make me feel less important than they are without my consent.

4

KEEPING YOUR EMOTIONS IN CHECK

"I DON'T WANT TO BE AT THE MERCY OF MY EMOTIONS. I WANT TO USE THEM, TO ENJOY THEM, AND TO DOMINATE THEM."

— OSCAR WILDE

I want for you what Oscar Wilde wished for himself: I want you to be able to feel and understand your emotions and handle them well so that you're always in control. That's what we'll be looking at in this chapter ... and it starts with getting back to basics and understanding what emotions actually are.

EMOTIONS 101

People often think that emotions are feelings, but they're actually two separate things. Your emotions are physiological states, most commonly generated as responses to events that either happen within you or outside of you. Your feelings, on the other hand, are the way you experience those emotions. Unlike emotions, they don't happen automatically. They're prompted by your conscious thoughts. Feelings don't happen without emotions, but it's possible to have emotions without feelings.

For example: A student receives a bad grade on a test, which triggers the emotion of disappointment. However, the student may choose to suppress or minimize their feelings of disappointment and focus on improving their performance instead.

THE SIX BASIC EMOTIONS

Due to ongoing debate amongst researchers, there's no consensus on the exact number of emotions. However, in a study published in the *Proceedings of the National Academy of Sciences in 2017,* researchers identified 27 distinct categories of emotion based on responses from over 800 participants who viewed a wide range of visual stimuli designed to elicit emotional responses. Those categories were amusement, anger, anxiety, awe, contentment, desire, disgust, envy, excitement, fear, gratitude, guilt, happiness, hate, hope, interest, joy, love, pleasure, pride, relief, sadness, satisfaction, shame, surprise, sympathy, and triumph.

The concept of basic emotions refers to a set of emotions that are considered to be universally experienced and recognized across different cultures and societies. The specific list varies, but the most commonly cited basic emotions are:

- anger
- fear
- happiness

- sadness
- surprise
- disgust

These six emotions are often referred to as the "basic" or "primary" emotions because they're thought to be innate, and they provide the foundation for a wide range of more complex emotions and behaviors.

Emotions are unconscious and affect the way we think. Imagine you're watching a scary movie in your room. Logically, you know you're safe, but you might still feel frightened. Your body will react, increasing your heart rate and maybe making you sweat. This is your autonomic nervous system kicking into action, and it often happens before you even become aware of your fear. Your emotions can influence your thoughts, so as your autonomic nervous system responds to the movie, you might start to become aware that you're feeling nervous. Suddenly every creak or bang in the house is scary and overrides your logical thought that you're safe.

WHY DO WE NEED EMOTIONS?

Essentially, your emotions are setting the stage for the thoughts you'll have, which might seem like a bad idea, but it's actually very helpful—your emotions help you to survive, avoid danger, make decisions, and understand others. We're affected by the emotions of those around us too, and that's because they give us information. For example, if your friend's facial expressions suddenly show fear, you're immediately going to start looking for danger nearby. Similarly, if you can tell that someone else is happy, you're going to feel safe and comfortable.

IDENTIFYING YOUR EMOTIONS

Being able to identify your emotions will help you to understand what's motivating your thoughts, actions, and feelings, and it will help you stay in control of them. There are four steps to this process, and they all start with asking yourself a question.

1. WHAT AM I FEELING?

Pay attention to what you're feeling, and try not to pass judgment on it. No emotion is good or bad, so there's no reason to beat yourself up for having any of them. This can be difficult at first, but as you do it more, you'll find it easier to recognize your emotions.

2. WHERE AM I FEELING IT?

Pay attention to where in your body you're experiencing your emotion. Your instinct may be to disconnect yourself from it if it's difficult to experience, but this is an opportunity to connect with it and understand it. If you're struggling with Step 1, this can help you to clarify what your emotion is. For example, if your fists are clenched, perhaps the emotion you're feeling is anger; if you have a lump in your throat, maybe you're experiencing sadness. Bear in mind that you can have a few emotions going on at once.

3. WHY AM I FEELING IT?

Emotions aren't always rational. It may be that you can clearly see you're having an emotional response to something that's happening right now, but it could be that your emotion is the result of a past experience. Stay with the emotion, and see if you can follow it back to its root. Pay attention to what you're thinking—this can be a clue.

4. WHAT DO I NEED?

Continue to focus on the emotion, paying attention to where you feel it and why it's happening. Can you work out what would help? For example, if you're angry, would it help you to walk away from the situation?

UNDERSTANDING YOUR EMOTIONS

Being able to identify your emotions is all well and good, but unless you understand them, it's only going to get you so far. When we're led by our emotions, we can make snap decisions that aren't necessarily good for us in the long run; however, if we can understand how they make us think and feel, we can make more informed decisions.

RECOGNIZE EMOTIONAL THINKING

We can recognize our emotions by paying attention to how they affect our thinking. If you notice yourself doing any of the following things, you're probably being led by your emotions, so it's worth taking a step back and thinking about your reaction.

- jumping to conclusions before you know all the information

- thinking in black and white without considering the complexities of a situation

- having paranoid thoughts

- overreacting and assuming the worst (often known as catastrophizing)

- making irrational decisions without considering the situation carefully

- making judgments quickly based on your feelings rather than the facts

PRACTICE SELF-COMPASSION

It's easy to judge yourself harshly, but by being compassionate toward yourself, you will create a safe space in which you can look at the emotions behind your thoughts and feelings. Of course, that's easier said than done, and if you've no idea what being compassionate toward yourself looks like, don't worry—try this exercise:

- Think of one challenge you want to focus on. For example: *Answering questions in class without feeling nervous or embarrassed.*

- Write down the situation. Try to be objective—in other words, try to write it from an outside perspective without bringing your own thoughts and judgments into it. For example: *When I'm asked a question in class, I struggle to think of the answer, and I get so nervous that I can't answer properly.*

- Pay attention to any emotions or sensations in your body that come up. Don't engage with them; just look at them openly and notice what they are. Write them down. *For example: I feel nervous. My heart rate speeds up, and I get hot and uncomfortable. My mind goes blank.*

- Next to each one, write down a supportive statement. Think of something you might say to your friend if they were in this situation. *For example: It's ok to feel nervous. You know the answers—you're just struggling to find them on the spot.*

- Recognize that it's natural to feel what you're feeling.

- Think of other people around the world who may be experiencing the same thing (it's often easier to be compassionate towards other people than it is to be compassionate towards ourselves).

- Extend yourself the compassion you might feel towards someone else in the same situation.

DISCUSS YOUR FEELINGS

Talking about how you feel is incredibly helpful. It gives you a sense of control, and it helps you see things from a different perspective. Try talking your problem through with a friend or someone in your family. Chances are, the person you're talking to has felt this way before too. It's not always easy to have these deep emotional conversations, so I like to go for a walk at the same time; it gives me something else I can focus on while I talk. That might work for you too, or you might like to try something else—playing a video game with someone while you're talking to them, for example, or playing a sport.

REFLECTING AND EVALUATING

It's never fun to revisit difficult emotions after they've passed, but doing so can help us to deal with them when they come up in the future. Here's an exercise you can try to practice doing that:

1. Think about the situations you've faced throughout the day.

2. How did you handle them? Did you act according to logic, or was your reaction based on emotional thinking?

3. Could you have done anything different to handle the situation better?

4. Imagine someone you're close to watching the situation. What would they think about how you reacted?

Asking yourself these questions can help you recognize your emotions and understand how they influence your thoughts and actions. From there, you can make changes to make your reactions better next time.

CONTROLLING YOUR EMOTIONS

Now, you can really start to take control and use your understanding of your emotions to guide your actions. This will help you in your relationships and daily social interactions, and it will help you to make good decisions and take care of yourself when you need to.

AIM FOR CONTROL (NOT REPRESSION)

Although you don't want your emotions to be in charge, it's equally important not to bury them. When you repress your emotions, the effect is that you stop yourself from feeling and expressing those feelings. Trust me; you don't want to go down that road. It can put both your mental and physical health at risk, potentially leading to depression, anxiety, stress, difficulty sleeping, and pain or tension in your muscles. The sweet spot is being able to get control of your emotions without hiding them from yourself.

ACCEPTING YOUR EMOTIONS

Accepting your emotions allows you to experience and recognize your feelings without trying to control or repress them. It involves recognizing that emotions are a natural and normal part of being human and that all emotions, even uncomfortable or difficult ones, serve a purpose and provide valuable information about our inner experiences and needs. Accepting your emotions will help you cultivate self-awareness, emotional resilience, compassion, and a better understanding of yourself and others.

To illustrate this point, imagine you're grieving because you just lost your beloved dog. Rather than attempting to suppress your feelings or push them away, you allow yourself to feel sad, recognizing that it's a normal and natural reaction to loss. You spend time reflecting on the good times you had with your dog, the lessons you can take from your experience, and how you can look after yourself at this difficult time. By accepting your sadness and working through it healthily, you'll begin to heal and move forward with greater self-awareness and emotional strength.

Keep A Journal

Perhaps you're an avid journaler, or perhaps the idea of writing about how you feel every day is about as appealing as jumping into an ice bath. Either way, it's worth thinking about how it can help you. Remember that there's no right or wrong way to journal. The most important thing is to find a technique that works for you and that you enjoy. When you write your feelings down and consider how they make you act, you give yourself an opportunity to spot the patterns— and when you do that, you can come up with ways to manage them better.

The Power Of A Deep Breath

Taking a deep breath won't stop you from having emotions, but remember, that's not what we're aiming for. What it can do is ground you and give you a little distance so that you can avoid triggering an extreme reaction in yourself. The next time you're feeling an intense emotion, try the following steps:

1. Inhale slowly. Imagine your breath rising up from deep down inside you.

2. Hold your breath while you count up to three, and then exhale slowly.

3. Repeat this phrase to yourself as though it were a mantra: "I am calm."

When It's Ok To Express Yourself ... And When It's Not

You don't want to repress your emotions, but it's also important to know whether or not it's an appropriate time to express them. There are situations when outbursts of strong emotions are reasonable and even expected—when your favorite team wins the game, for example. But there are others where it will do you more harm than good. Screaming at your teacher because they've unfairly given you detention isn't going to help your situation. The trick is to be aware of your surroundings and sit with your feelings until you can get to an appropriate place to let them out.

TAKING TIME AND SPACE FOR YOURSELF

When you're experiencing intense emotion, it's often helpful to get some distance so that you can be sure that your reactions are reasonable. This could be done by physically distancing yourself—walking away from a distressing situation, for example—or it could be done by using a distraction to give yourself some mental distance. Be careful with this one; you don't want to distract yourself so much that you ignore your feelings, and it's important to come back to them when you're ready to deal with them. There are plenty of healthy distractions you could try. My favorites are going for a walk, watching comedy, and talking to a friend, but you could try anything you like as long as it's only a temporary distraction.

MANAGING STRESS

When we're stressed, managing our emotions can be even more difficult than usual—no matter how good at it we normally are. You can reduce your stress by making sure you get enough sleep, spending time with your friends, exercising regularly, spending time on your favorite hobbies, getting outside in nature, and meditating.

MEDITATION

Meditating can improve your awareness of your experiences and feelings, and every time you do it, you learn more about how to sit with your feelings and pay attention to them without pushing them away.

You can read more about meditation (and find plenty of exercises to try, too) in my other book, *Social Anxiety Workbook for Teens*. So, for now, we'll keep it simple. If you're new to meditation and want to give it a go, try this exercise:

Sit somewhere comfortable and quiet, and focus on your breathing. Start with 5 or 10 minutes, and try to work your way up to 20 minutes a day. Keep your attention focused on your breath, and pay attention to any thoughts and feelings that emerge. Observe them without judgment, and if your attention wanders, gently bring it back to focus on your breathing.

If you want to go even further, try this meditation, which is specifically designed to help you with difficult emotions:

1. Sit somewhere comfortable and quiet. Think of something hard you're going through, and recognize your wish to push it away.

2. Take deep breaths, breathing in through your nose and out through your mouth. Visualize a figure coming into your mind—a strong, compassionate being who holds you in love, security, and acceptance.

3. Now turn your attention to your problem. There's no need to be afraid; you're safe in the arms of the compassionate figure. Visualize them speaking kindly to you, telling you you're not alone and that you're going to be ok. Repeat these statements as often as you need to hear them, and feel your mind and body slow down.

4. When you feel yourself pushing your emotions away, turn yourself gently back toward them. By training yourself to acknowledge and accept the difficulty, you're helping yourself to feel it as less of a challenge.

5. You may find it helpful to hold a comforting object while you do this.

Emotions aren't always easy, but none of them are wrong. The goal is to be able to handle them without allowing them to take control of you. In the next chapter, we'll look at how you can do the same thing with time—so you're always the one in charge of your experience. First things first, though: Here's your affirmation for this chapter:

I acknowledge my emotions and allow myself to feel them.

5
BECOME THE MASTER OF TIME

"TIME MANAGEMENT IS A SUPERPOWER. YOU CAN ACHIEVE ANYTHING WHEN YOU LEARN TO HARNESS ITS POTENTIAL."

— ROBIN SHARMA

You have more control over time than you think ... but only if you have the necessary skills.

Mastering time management is like having a super-power to unlock rewards and maximize productivity, even if time travel isn't possible. Do let me know if you figure that out, though!

THE IMPORTANCE OF TIME MANAGEMENT

Time management is a prerequisite for success in all areas of life. Whether you're a student, a worker, or just trying to balance multiple responsibilities, effectively managing your time makes a huge difference. When you prioritize your tasks and allocate time for each one, you'll be able to get more done in less time. This means you'll have more free time to do things you enjoy, reduce stress, and increase productivity. Plus, you'll be less likely to procrastinate and miss deadlines.

But time management isn't just about being efficient; it's also about setting goals and working toward them. You'll be more motivated and focused when you have a clear plan for achieving your goals. Stay tuned—we'll cov-er this later in the chapter. We'll also look at scheduling, breaking tasks down into manageable chunks, and eliminating distractions. It may take some practice, but once you master the art of time management, like Sia, you'll be unstoppable!

TIME MANAGEMENT: THE BASICS

Time management is the act of planning and organizing your time so that you can get everything done, even when the pressure's on. Every high achiever you can think of manages their time well, and the good news is that it's a skill you can easily train yourself in. If you're not great at it yet, don't worry—that's perfectly normal for teenagers, and with a bit of practice, you'll level up in no time.

HOW TO MANAGE YOUR TIME LIKE A PRO

It will take time and practice to truly become the master of your own time. Work on each of these points consistently enough, and you'll find yourself getting better and better.

PRIORITIZATION

You'll get more done when you focus your time on the most important things. The trick is to know what they are. One way to do this is to use the Eisenhower Matrix, which, I'm sorry to tell you, is far less interesting than it sounds! The basic idea is that some things are important, and some things are urgent. Important things are tasks that lead to you achieving your goals, and urgent things are tasks that require your attention straight away. Usually, they're more about someone else's goals than they are about your own, and you're more likely to focus on them because there'll be some kind of consequence if you don't.

The idea of the Eisenhower Matrix is that by recognizing which tasks are which, you'll enable yourself to focus on the important ones rather than spending all your time on the urgent ones, and that will mean you'll be able to make progress rather than constantly spending your time on things that don't matter to you in the long run.

To put the Eisenhower Matrix into practice, make a list of all the tasks and activities you have to do. Then put each activity into one of the following four categories:

1. **Important and Urgent** (These are the tasks to focus on first.)

2. **Important but Not Urgent** (Make sure you have plenty of time to do these tasks well so that they don't become urgent and you end up having to rush them.)

3. **Urgent but Not Important** (These usually come from other people, and you'll have more control over them once you leave school. You don't have much power when it comes to arguing with teachers!) Later in life, you can manage these tasks by delegating and declining requests.

4. **Neither Urgent Nor Important** (These are generally just distractions, and the best thing to do is avoid or cancel them.)

SCHEDULING

Knowing what you need to do is one thing, but timing is crucial as well. Have you ever noticed that hard things are easier to do in the morning before you've had time to worry about them? Use that to your advantage—make the things you least want to do the things you get out of the way first. Use a calendar or a planner to keep a note of how you'll use your time, what your priorities are, and when you need to get things done. Do this for long enough, and it will become a habit that will serve you for a lifetime.

CONCENTRATION

Setting aside time to dedicate to the most important things is a good first step, but unless you use that time well, it won't serve you. Whenever you're working on a task, do your best to minimize distractions. Put your phone away (shock, horror!), turn the TV off, and focus. I find I work best in short chunks of time. Consider setting a timer and making a deal with yourself: If you work solidly for 20 minutes, you can reward yourself with 5 minutes of checking social media. You can still have that distraction; you're just going to plan for it instead of letting it interrupt your flow. Focus on one thing at a time. Trying to get everything done at once might seem like you'll get everything done more quickly, but you'll be much more productive if you complete one thing before moving on to the next.

WAKE UP EARLIER

I know what you're thinking. Something along the lines of, "Noooooooo!" That's okay—there's a very good reason for this. When you're a teenager, your body secretes melatonin (the hormone that governs your sleep) between about 11 pm and 8 am. That's why you find it hard to go to sleep early and virtually impossible to wake up early. This will change as you get older, and when it does, getting up earlier will help you get a head start on your to-do list, and you'll probably find you're more productive in the morning too. That said, not everyone is a morning person, and something you can work with right now while your hormones make it difficult is to identify the time of day that you're most productive. If you get home from school feeling energized, it might be best for you to do your homework straight away. If you find you're exhausted at that time, it might be better for you to rest a bit, go for a walk and wind down, then come back to your homework after dinner. There's no right answer—you have to find what works for you.

USE APPS

There's an app for everything nowadays, and time management is no exception. You can find planners, timers, and apps to help you stay focused and block distractions. Search the app store and see what's available, but if you'd like a couple of good ones to get started with, I recommend the **myHomework** student planner for managing your schedule and **StayFocused** for blocking websites that distract you from your work (don't worry—you can unblock them when you're done!)

THE 80/20 RULE

You may have heard of this by its other name, the Pareto Principle. The idea is that 80% of results come from 20% of actions—in other words, 80% of the work you create comes from only 20% of the time you spend working on it. When you focus on the most important tasks, you can spend less time working and still see the same output. When you get this right, it can feel like you just cracked the code to the secret bonus level! This comes back to prioritization again. It's those top priorities that will bring you the most significant results, and you'll have more time to spend on the things you love doing too.

BREAK TASKS INTO MANAGEABLE CHUNKS

Have you ever looked at a piece of homework or the mess in your room and been so overwhelmed by how much there is to do that you don't know where to start? A good way to deal with this is to break those big over-whelming tasks into smaller chunks. First, identify what tasks you have, and work out which one is your priority. Then, break that task down into steps—what different subtasks are needed to complete it? Are there any that need to be done first in order to complete the next? (For example, an art project might require you to gather supplies before you can do anything else.) Each step is a milestone, and your next job is to schedule each one. So, looking at our example, on Day 1 of that art project, you might gather your supplies; on Day 2, you might draw the outline; and on Days 3 and 4, you might paint. That art project may have seemed daunting at first, but now it's much more manageable.

REGROUP EVERY WEEK

No matter how organized you are, there will always be some weeks when things just don't go to plan. The trick is to regroup at the end of the week, catching up on anything that got missed and planning for the week ahead. Perhaps you'll find that some things have to carry over into the next week, but that's ok because you know about them, and you can work them into your schedule.

GOAL SETTING

In his book, *Upgrade Yourself: Simple Strategies to Transform Your Mindset, Improve Your Habits and Change Your Life*, Thibaut Meurisse said, "Each time you tell yourself you'll do something but don't, your self-esteem suffers. If you do it repeatedly, the empty promises you make to yourself lose their power. If you know that whatever you promise won't get done, what's the point in making promises to yourself?" He was highlighting this for a particular reason, going on to say that "Breaking promises to yourself will ultimately cause you to stop setting goals." So why is that a problem?

Setting yourself goals is key to managing your time well, and achieving them is good for your self-esteem. It requires you to understand what you want to achieve, but if you know this, it can be incredibly motivating and give you a sense of purpose.

Goals are what you want to achieve in the long run, and within each goal, there's a set of objectives that you'll need to achieve in order to reach that goal. Breaking tasks down into manageable chunks will help you with this—it's essentially the same thing we looked at in time management but on a smaller scale. To set a goal, you'll need to break it down into its objectives and set deadlines for when you want to achieve them.

This is all well and good, but why is goal setting so important? I'm glad you asked!

- It makes you focus your attention on tasks that will help you achieve your ambitions rather than wasting it on distractions.

- It pushes you to work harder because you want to achieve a particular outcome.

- You're more likely to persevere when you're faced with setbacks.

- It allows you to reflect on habits and behaviors that are either helping or hindering you from achieving your goals. This is great for personal growth.

- It enables you to prioritize and focus on the things that are most important, making better use of your time and making success more likely.

- It motivates you and makes you more likely to hold yourself accountable. If you want to enter a race, for example, you're more likely to train than you would be if you didn't have the race as a goal to work towards.

- It builds resilience. You're more likely to work out strategies for overcoming obstacles when they're standing in the way of something you're determined to achieve. Setbacks provide an opportunity for learning and personal growth, and as you work through them, you'll build up your resilience.

- It gives you a clear roadmap to follow, giving you new insights and points of view along the way that will challenge you to grow and develop as a person. It prompts you to reflect on your strengths and weaknesses and find ways to improve and challenge yourself.

SMART GOALS

If you end up working for a big company when you're older, you'll probably find that they work with SMART goals, so coming to grips with them now will stand you in good stead. The principle is that a SMART goal is:

- **Specific:** It lays out exactly what you want to achieve.

- **Measurable:** You can track your progress, and you'll know when you've achieved it.

- **Attainable:** Achieving it is possible.

- **Relevant:** It's in line with your interests and any other goals you may have.

- **Timely:** It includes firm deadlines.

Consider the difference between these two goals:

1. Get good grades.

2. Get an A on my history essay.

Goal 1 is general and vague. It applies to every class you take, and it's not clear what you have to do to reach it. Goal 2 is specific, attainable, and relevant, with a clear deadline, and you'll be able to track your progress along your way to reaching it.

SMART goals are great motivators, and they make it easy to achieve what you set out to do. Let's say you want to start a writing group at your school. What would a SMART goal for this look like?

- **Specific:** I want to start a writing group that will publish a school magazine.

- **Measurable:** It will have 6+ members and will publish a magazine each term.

- **Attainable:** My school will allow this, and by meeting two lunchtimes a week, we will be able to produce enough material to fill a magazine every term.

- **Relevant:** I love writing, and I would like a career as a journalist.

- **Timely:** There is a term deadline built into the goal.

Try setting a SMART goal for something you've been struggling to motivate yourself to do. I'm willing to bet that it'll make that impossible-looking task a whole lot more achievable.

ORGANIZATIONAL SKILLS

It might be surprising to think that your physical organization would have anything to do with time management, but it's more relevant than most people realize. When we're disorganized, we're more easily distracted, and we're more likely to get stressed. We don't perform as well, and we lose time searching for what we need and are unable to focus. I have to confess that I had to train myself to become organized—it didn't come naturally to me. But the good news is that this is possible, and even if your organizational skills make you look like a mad scientist, you can turn that around. Here's how you can get started:

- **Recognize the difference between tidy and messy.** That might sound simple, but do you really know what tidy looks like? It isn't just all your books and papers stuffed in drawers so that you have a clear desk. It's the books lined up on shelves where you can easily find them and the papers filed neatly in folders and put away systematically.

- **Use designated spaces.** Think in categories, and designate specific places where you'll keep important items. You might keep your school work on your desk, for example, and the things you need for your morning routine on the vanity table.

- **Start with a clean space.** Amazingly enough, our brains work better in clear spaces. When your desk is a mess, your focus will be worse. Start every work session with five minutes of cleaning up your desk, putting away distractions, and keeping the things you need near to hand.

- **Prepare the night before.** Write yourself a reminder list that tells you what to do at the end of each day to prepare for the next. Everyone's list will look a little different, but it might contain things like, "Pack a lunch," "Pack all the books I need for school," "Put my pencil case back in my bag," and "Prepare my clothes for the next day."

- **Use a checklist.** Write down all the cleaning and organizational tasks you have for the week. Divide them up according to which ones need to be completed daily and which ones should be done on specific days. Keep the checklist somewhere that you'll easily see it, and refer to it every day.

- **Use the OHIO rule.** No, you needn't go to Cleveland! OHIO stands for "Only Handle It Once," and it will help you to stay on top of the tasks you need to complete. It means answering an email as soon as you open it rather than coming back to it another time or completing your homework in one sitting. It makes you much more productive, I can tell you.

- **Know when you're overloaded.** No matter how organized you are, sometimes you'll get overwhelmed. The key is knowing when your strategies aren't working and your organization is taking a knock. When you feel yourself getting overloaded, take a break, go back to your organizational system, and start again.

7 STEPS TO BEING ORGANIZED

If organizing yourself still seems daunting and you feel like I've just asked you to climb Everest, try following these seven steps:

Know what you need to do. If you struggle to remember what you need to get done, lists are your friends. Personally, I have two lists—a long-term list and a daily task list.

Plan when to do it. Your brain will worry about tasks left undone, but you can get around this by knowing when you're going to do them. As soon as that piece of homework is on your Monday night to- do list, your brain will stop worrying about when it's going to get done.

Give yourself space and time. You can't organize yourself if you don't have time to do it. Allocate some time every day to plan for what you need to do the next day.

Know what's important and what's urgent. Revisit this section of the chapter if you need a reminder.

Break your tasks down into manageable chunks. Again, go back up the chapter to remind yourself how to do this.

Expect extra tasks. Sometimes, you'll have to do something that you didn't plan for. Try not to get frustrated; just see whether you can move anything off today's list and get it done tomorrow instead. And if not, you know you need to renegotiate your deadline.

Keep on top of it. Even if you really want to do something else, try to stay on task. The risk if you don't is that your schedule will get messed up, and it'll have a ripple effect on the rest of the week.

No matter how hard you try, sometimes things will get in the way of your organization and time management planning. Two of the biggest of these are unexpected problems that arise and decisions you have to make. We're going to look at how you can deal with those in the next chapter ... But first, it's time for that affirmation. It's a good one to repeat to yourself whenever you're feeling overwhelmed, and guess what? It's true!

I can achieve anything I want to. Success is within my power.

KNOWLEDGE SHARED IS A PROBLEM SOLVE

"SHARING KNOWLEDGE IS THE MOST FUNDAMENTAL ACT OF FRIENDSHIP. BECAUSE IT IS A WAY YOU CAN GIVE SOMETHING WITHOUT LOSING SOMETHING."

— RICHARD STALLMAN

Before we get to how to approach solving problems, let's address one you may well face as you uplevel your life skills: You're one step ahead of some of your friends.

Imagine you've been asked to work on a group presentation at school. You're organized, you have clear goals for your role, and you've planned exactly how you're going to use your time to get everything done well in advance of the presentation.

And then you learn that your friend has done nothing. He knows what his role is; he knows what he's meant to be researching; he knows how he's meant to fit it into the presentation. But it's two days before the deadline, and you know he hasn't done a thing.

You're ready, you're chill, and you're eager to rehearse the presentation ... But you can't because not all of it is there. Suddenly you don't feel so chill anymore ...

It's not your friend's fault ... He hasn't acquired these life skills yet. Perhaps you could point him in the direction of this book—that'll help. And you can help other kids too.

By leaving a review of this book on Amazon, you'll show other young people where they can find everything they need to boost their life skills and their social skills so that they're as ready as you are to tackle the adult world.

Simply by letting other readers know how this book has helped you and what they'll find inside, you'll show them where they can find the lessons that school will never teach—and arguably, they're the most important skills of all.

Thank you for your help in getting the word out. If you're not sure what to do, ask your parents or guardians to lead you through the review process (another life skill!). All young people deserve to have this knowledge—and you can help me get it to them.

To do that, simply scan this QR code or click the link below. These proprietary pathways will lead you directly to the official Amazon page, where you can effortlessly locate your cherished book order and access the esteemed "Write a Review" button.
Once completed a thank you window will pop up on your screen and later you will receive an email from Amazon to confirm that your review has been posted. Embrace the opportunity to leave a lasting legacy within our realm of cherished literary works.

https://geni.us/writeabookreview

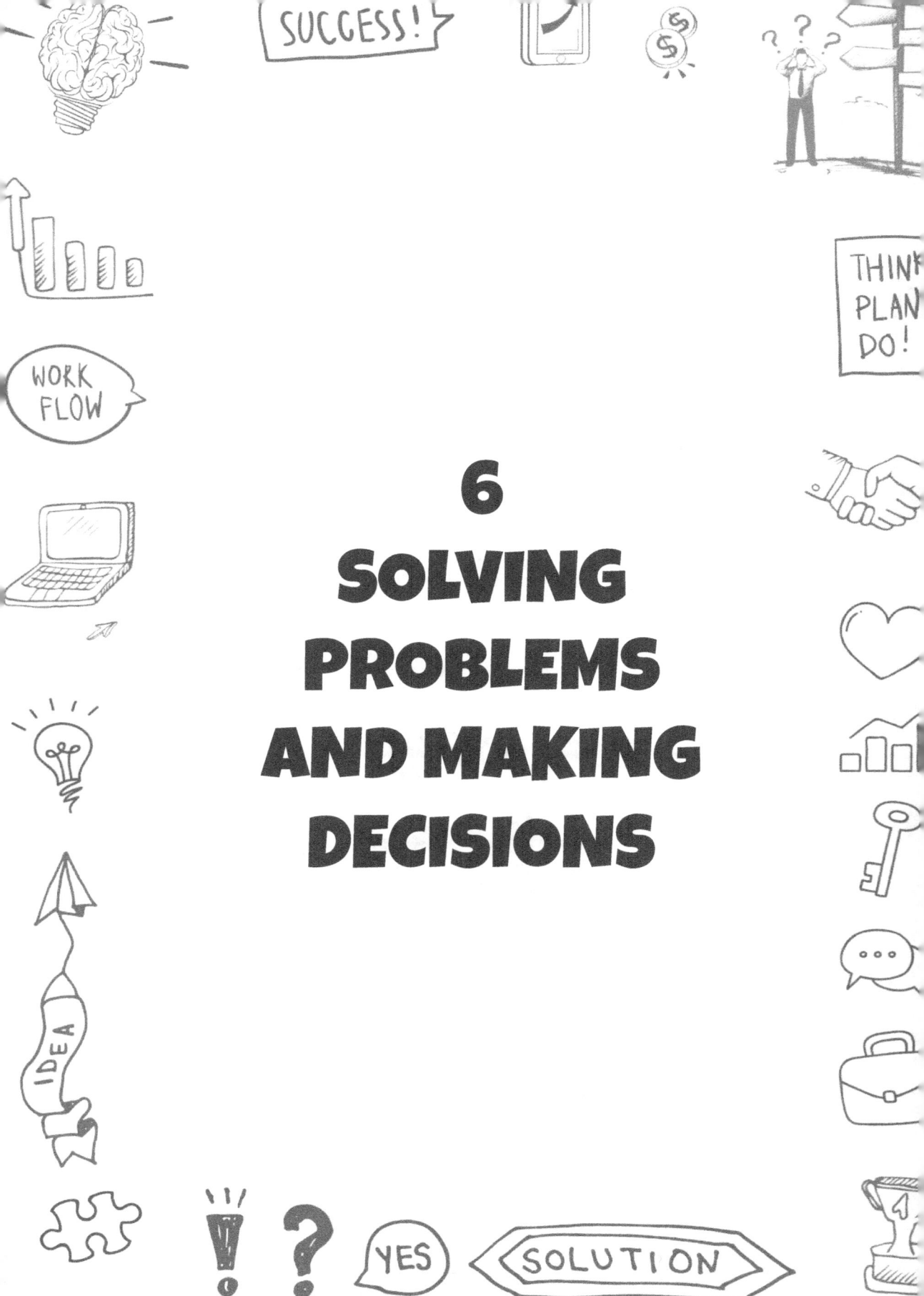

6
SOLVING PROBLEMS AND MAKING DECISIONS

"EVERY PROBLEM IS A GIFT. WITHOUT THEM, WE WOULDN'T GROW."

— TONY ROBBINS

No one likes having problems, but without the need to find solutions, we wouldn't be able to grow as individuals. Sometimes unexpected challenges can disrupt your plans, but they can also help you develop new skills. In the end, you may look back and see that the difficulty was beneficial. The secret is adopting a "growth mindset." It sounds intimidating, doesn't it? Let's take a look at what it means.

DEVELOPING A GROWTH MINDSET

Nowadays, we're taught that everyone is born with their own set of qualities and quirks. Some kids are smart, some have ADHD, some are quiet or loud, some are good at music or math, some might be lazy, others hard workers, and some get in trouble a lot. Grown-ups like parents and teachers use labels to describe kids based on these things. When we're young, the things that are said about us have a profound impact and ultimately shape who we believe we are. That's how our identity is first formed, and it affects how we behave and what kind of life we create.

For instance, if we believe we're introverted, we may choose not to speak up in social situations. Over time, this reinforces our self-image and further entrenches our sense of identity. Developing a growth mindset involves being aware of how our actions affect our self-perception, and we must take steps to change our behavior if we want to create a different reality for ourselves. Think of J.K. Rowling. The Harry Potter series was rejected by many publishers before she finally saw success, but she always believed in herself and didn't let those failures put her off.

But what if you have the complete opposite personality? This is called a fixed mindset. It's cool to be yourself as long as it helps you live the life you want. But sometimes, we want more and bigger things, which can create a problem when who we are right now doesn't match up with who we want to be. This can be really frustrating and confusing, and it's called a mental block. You believe that your abilities are set in stone and that you can't improve. This leads to lower achievement because it makes you search for easy ways without challenging yourself. In the end, you find it difficult to deal with failure because you haven't built up the resilience that having a growth mindset gives you. People with a fixed mindset tend to avoid challenges and only do things they're already good at, which limits their belief that they'll ever get better. It's like the cartoon character Homer Simpson from *The Simpsons* versus Félicie from *Leap*.

"How do I get out of this rat wheel?" you might ask. The answer's surprisingly simple: Get rid of the idea that you're always going to be the same, and focus on growing and improving yourself.

PROBLEM-SOLVING SKILLS

Whether it's figuring out how to approach an essay, trying to mend a broken phone, or solving a problem in a friendship, life will always have its problems. Think of the last time you were faced with a problem. How did you feel? Perhaps you felt overwhelmed, under pressure, stressed out, and anxious; maybe you were frustrated with yourself or others. Did you find it hard to concentrate, or feel tired and confused? Or maybe you were excited by the challenge. All of these feelings are common reactions to a problem or situation. Being able to solve them will help you get what you want and gain a sense of control. Later in life, potential employers will want to know that you have the necessary skills to approach a problem confidently and look for solutions, so picking up these skills now will serve you well. Let's start by looking at the steps needed to solve a problem.

STEP 1: IDENTIFY THE PROBLEM

Be as specific as possible when finding a solution to a problem. Look closely at the issue: Is it general, big, small, or crucial? Work on each element individually, and get to the core of the problem. For example, you may say, "I hate my school." There could be various issues beneath the surface that make you feel this way, and breaking them down will mean you can identify them and look for solutions. You might find that math class is too easy, or maybe you have a problematic teacher or there is someone in your history class who's causing you trouble. By listing the different ways the problem affects you, you can better understand what you're dealing with and start working toward diminishing it.

STEP 2: WORK OUT THE GOALS FOR EACH PROBLEM

Once you've identified your problems, it's time to figure out what you want. Ask yourself these questions:

- What can I do to resolve the issue?

- What do I want and need?

- How can I make those things happen while still being mindful of others?

Make sure your answers are realistic and things that are actually within your control. It's no use wishing that your problematic teacher will disappear, but what you can do is come up with a strategy to help you cope with them. For each of the problems you identified in Step 1, ask each of the questions above to get a clear idea of what you need.

STEP 3: BRAINSTORM SOLUTIONS

The next goal is to find as many possible solutions as you can. Don't worry if some of your ideas are a bit wild—there'll be time to hone them later. The goal is to think of as many realistic options as you can. Let's go back to the problematic teacher. A list of solutions might look something like this:

- I can sit at the back of the class, away from his/her desk.

- I can make sure I'm really polite when I talk to him/her.

- I can ask my parents to talk to him/her.

- I can keep my head down and get on with my work —class is only an hour.

- I can be rude to him/her and hope I am transferred to another class.

- I can ask to switch to another class.

- I can change schools.

Obviously, not all of those strategies are winners. In fact, some are downright bad ideas. However, the goal at this stage is to come up with as many solutions as you can without judging them.

STEP 4: RULE OUT THE BAD IDEAS

Now it's time to analyze all your solutions and get rid of the ones that are either impossible or going to make your life more difficult. Think about the potential outcomes of each situation to help you decide. Let's go back to our list from the last step:

- I can sit at the back of the class, away from his/her desk.

- I can make sure I'm really polite when I talk to him/her.

- I can ask my parents to talk to him/her. *This could escalate the situation or draw unwanted attention to you.*

- I can keep my head down and get on with my work—class is only an hour.

- I can be rude to him/her and hope I am transferred to another class. *He/she may not transfer you, and the result could be detention and an even worse relationship with him/her.*

- I can ask to switch to another class.

- I can change schools. *This is quite difficult and time- consuming, and you don't know that you'll get on with the teachers there either.*

STEP 5: CONSIDER THE PROS AND CONS OF THE REMAINING SOLUTIONS

Now that you only have reasonable options left, it's time to compare the solutions, thinking about the positive and negative outcomes that could result from each one. Let's go back to our list:

- I can sit at the back of the class, away from his/her desk.

Positive: He/she would be less likely to pick on me in class if I'm out of his/her line of sight.

Negative: I can't hear so well from the back of the room, so I might not get as much out of the lesson.

- I can make sure I'm really polite when I talk to him/her.

Positive: This might make him/her see me in a new light and treat me with more respect.

Negative: This might be really hard to do when he's/she's treating me unfairly.

- I can keep my head down and get on with my work—class is only an hour.

Positive: This way, I'll get the most out of my class, and there will be no unfortunate consequences.

Negative: I might still feel frustrated and not enjoy the class.

- I can ask to switch to another class.

Positive: This would mean I still get the most out of my lesson, and I wouldn't have to interact with this teacher anymore.

Negative: I might not be able to switch classes, and then my relationship with him/her might get worse.

STEP 6: IDENTIFY THE BEST OPTION

Now it's time to make a decision. Perhaps one solution stands out as being better than the others, or perhaps there are several you could implement at once. In the example of the problematic teacher, after comparing the pros and cons of each solution, the best option might be to keep your head down and get on with your work while also trying to be more polite to that teacher.

STEP 7: IMPLEMENT THE SOLUTION

This is where all that planning pays off. When your solution involves communicating with others, think back to the communication skills we talked about in Chapter 3 to make sure you approach the situation in a way that will get you the outcome you want.

STEP 8: REFLECT

You might think you're done at this point, but this last step is crucial to molding the way you'll deal with a similar problem in the future. Once you've tried the solution out, review how it went. Did it work? If not, then you'll need to try another approach. If you feel it could have gone better, think about what you could do differently in the future.

BUILDING PROBLEM-SOLVING SKILLS

Tackling problems as they come up will certainly help you build your problem-solving skills, but you can also do this intentionally. Try deliberately taking on problems you enjoy—something like a video game, a lateral thinking puzzle, or Sudoku. Many things we enjoy doing in our free time contain problems that have to be approached logically, and this will help you hone your skills. Problems don't have to be mental either; maybe you'd prefer a physical challenge. Cooking, crafting, and DIY are good examples of physical tasks that often involve solving problems.

DECISION MAKING

If your goal is to make better decisions (which it should be!), the secret is to be fully informed. The more you know, the more power you'll have to be decisive—like a superhero with a crystal ball. Be careful to avoid getting stuck in analysis paralysis, though, because that's just like eating too much pizza—it'll make you feel overwhelmed and sluggish.

Let's zone in on a specific example. Imagine you're deciding whether to quit a music class right before a concert. Consider whether your decision will have an impact on anyone else. In this case, it may impact your parents, and it will certainly affect your classmates, so it's best to talk to them first. They might have some wisdom to share, or they might just tell you to stop being a ding-dong and do what's right. Most decisions can be reversed, but if others are involved, things get more complicated, and you end up feeling like you're trying to juggle flaming pineapples. The moral of the story? Don't rush your decision.

LOGIC VS. EMOTION

So let's say you have to make a decision about whether to stay in and study or go to a movie with your friends. Of course going to the movie is probably much more appealing than doing your homework, and if you're basing your decision on short-term happiness, it's a no-brainer. If you let your head get involved, though, you might look at the long- term goal of getting into the college you've chosen, and in this case, the long-term outcome of getting good grades might win. With a little thought, you can find a solution that satisfies both needs. Perhaps you go to the movie tonight, but you do your homework tomorrow morning when you had planned a lazy start. Or perhaps you persuade your friends to go to the movie tomorrow night, and you do homework tonight.

Logic and emotion both have a place. It's important to listen to what your feelings are telling you, but it would be unwise to act on them without taking a moment to think it through. It's not always easy to tell if you're acting with your head or your heart, though. The secret is to identify your feelings and think about where they're coming from and whether they're justified. When you use logic to check your feelings, you're more likely to understand your motivation and come to a smart decision. You may have to compromise, but it might be better than making an extreme decision in either direction.

STEPS TO MAKING A GOOD DECISION

To make decisions less daunting, try this five-step process. You'll notice that it's not that dissimilar from the process you followed in the prob-lem-solving section.

STEP 1: IDENTIFY THE CHOICE

Just as identifying the specific problem is key to solving it, understanding the decision you're facing is key to making an effective choice. Spell out the problem to yourself: "I'm deciding whether to stay in music class or drop out."

STEP 2: BRAINSTORM YOUR OPTIONS

List all the options you can think of—including the compromises. It may seem like it's a binary choice between staying in the class and dropping out, but delve under the surface, and you might see that you could remain in class for the rest of the term or drop out once the concert is over. Consider why you want to drop out. If you've decided you'd rather play a sport than learn an instrument and you don't have time for both, you'll probably need to drop the class. If, however, you'd prefer to play the piano than the clarinet, it might be worth asking your teacher if you can switch instruments.

STEP 3: CONSIDER THE PROS AND CONS OF EACH OUTCOME

Write down a list of pros and cons for each possible decision. This will help you to make your decision with logic rather than being driven only by your emotion. Let's keep going with the music class decision:

- Stay in class:

Pros: I won't let anyone down, my parents won't lose money, and I might start to enjoy it more.

Cons: I won't have time to do what I really want to do; I'll have to keep doing something I don't enjoy.

- Drop out of class:

Pros: I'll have time to do what I really want to; I can stop doing an activity I don't enjoy.

Cons: My classmates are relying on me for the concert; my parents have paid a lot of money for this class.

- Drop out of class at a later point:

Pros: I won't let my classmates down; my parents will lose less money. I'll soon have more time for the activity I'd rather do, and I'll get to finish what I've been practicing for

Cons: I'll have to keep doing something I don't enjoy for longer; I won't be able to do another activity for a while.

STEP 4: COME UP WITH A PLAN

Review the list you created in Step 3, and think about what actions you can take next. After looking at the pros and cons in our music class example, it seems like the best decision would be to delay dropping out until after the concert. To put that plan into action, you'll need to tell your parents and your music teacher what your decision is and reassure your friends that you'll still be there until after the concert.

STEP 5: REFLECT

Yep, it's that one again! Just as with problem-solving, reviewing your decision once you've made it will help you to learn from your mistakes and make better decisions in the future. Think about how it felt to make the decision and what happened as a result of it. Was there a compromise you could have made that would have led to a better outcome? Don't beat yourself up about a bad decision—just make a commitment to learn from your mistake.

Ok, that's enough problems and decisions for one book! We're going to take an about turn now and change topics entirely. Now, we're moving to all things driving. If you're too young to drive, you might still get something out of reading about what's ahead for you, but you can always skip this chapter and come back to it when it's relevant. First, though (Yep, you guessed it!), it's time for another affirmation:

I am confident that I can solve any problem life throws my way.

7

GETTING BEHIND THE WHEEL WITH CONFIDENCE

My colleague Victoria was reluctant to let her son Paul learn to drive, and she fought him on it whenever he would ask, thinking he just wanted to do it to feel more grown up. She regretted that later when she saw how beneficial it was. You may not have the opportunity to learn to drive for a while, and you may not even be old enough yet. But if you do get the chance, you'll find it offers a lot of value.

WHY LEARN TO DRIVE?

Learning to drive offers more than just the freedom to travel independently—it provides valuable opportunities for responsibility, job prospects, and financial savings. By demonstrating responsibility to your parents or guardians, you will earn their trust. Having a driver's license opens up part-time job options and expands possibilities for future full-time employment. Driving yourself to school eliminates reliance on buses or parental transportation, and it may enable you to assist with younger siblings' activities. Driving, rather than relying on public transport or ride-sharing services, is often cost-effective too. Surprisingly, driving also promotes brain growth through multitasking and developing neuroplasticity, as it requires coordinating various tasks simultaneously. You're training your brain to process a lot of information at once, and that's going to help you in all areas of your life.

THE HOW OF LEARNING TO DRIVE

Obtaining a driver's license is essential for legally operating a motor vehicle, but the minimum age for applying varies by country. Typically, it falls between 16 and 18 years of age, with the option to acquire a learner's permit at a younger age. With a learner's permit, you can drive under the supervision of a licensed adult or instructor until passing your driving test. Enrolling in a recognized driving school is often recommended (and even mandatory in some countries). After completing the required lessons, you can apply for a provisional license, which involves a driving skills test and a theory exam. The provisional license may have restrictions on passenger count and driving hours. The eligibility age for a full license differs depending on your location. It's important to research and follow the specific requirements of your country. When you apply to a driving school, they will provide precise information on the necessary steps and how to obtain the appropriate license.

Before You Learn to Drive

Prepare yourself for driving by familiarizing yourself with the inside of a car. Ask a family member who drives to help you find the seat, mirror, and steering wheel adjustments that suit you. Learn about dashboard controls, warning lights, indicators, windshield wipers, headlights, and safety features like seat belts and airbags. Practice starting the engine, using the handbrake, and operating the brake and gas pedals. If possible, ask your parents to take you to a quiet location (such as an empty parking lot) to practice driving forward, reversing, and turning. Don't worry if it takes you more than one attempt to get the hang of pedal pressure and steering—

it will become natural over time. During practice, focus on maintaining awareness of your surroundings by checking mirrors and scanning for hazards.

EARLY SKILLS TO MASTER

Once you're able to get out on the road, either with your driving instructor or someone in your family, the skills you'll need to pick up will come much more easily if you've already gotten a feel for the vehicle and practiced handling it. Your instructor will know what to teach you, but it's helpful to be aware of the skills you'll need. Here's what you'll need to practice:

- making turns safely at the correct speed and with the use of signals

- gradually coming to a stop and braking smoothly

- steadily increasing your speed (within the speed limit)

- what to do at stop signs and lights recognizing who has the right of way

- driving on roads with both single lanes and multiple lanes

- changing lanes safely

- maintaining a steady speed and keeping a safe distance from the vehicle in front of you

- checking for and recognizing hazards

- driving in school zones and other areas with lower speed limits

- sharing road space with buses, cyclists, and pedestrians

- reacting appropriately to an emergency vehicle

As with most things in life, it's practice that makes perfect, so try to get out on the road as often as you can. Begin in areas with low speed limits and low traffic—your parents or driving instructor will know where these are.

Once you get further through your training and you've mastered these early skills, you can level up by driving in areas with higher speed limits and more traffic, as well as adding the following skills to your repertoire:

- merging into moving traffic

- identifying exits and interpreting road signs

- using toll booths

- overtaking other vehicles (and being overtaken)

- showing courtesy to other drivers

USING THE HIGHWAY

I remember the first time I ever drove on a multi-lane highway, and I have to admit, it scared me. This is perfectly normal, and the best thing you can do is rip the band-aid off as soon as you're ready. Ask your parents to take you during a time of day when it's quieter, and it will be easier to merge into traffic. Have a few goes during these quieter periods before trying busier times. Driving on the highway is a bit different from driving on other roads. You'll need to practice the following skills:

- using longer stopping distances (due to the higher speed limit)

- checking your blind spots before merging or changing lanes

- driving alongside large trucks

- reading signs to prepare for interchanges

- being aware of stopped or slow traffic in front of you

It might seem like a lot to begin with, but the more you practice, the more it will feel like second nature—I promise!

LOOKING AFTER YOUR CAR

You might think that once you've got your license, you're good to go, but driving is only part of the story. To be fully prepared for adulthood (and for anything that might happen to you on the road before you get there), you need to know how to look after your car too. Here are the essentials:

TIRES

Your tires are essential to your car operating safely. Did you know that a car with tires underinflated by over 25% has a three times higher likelihood of being involved in an accident? The easiest way to check your inflation is to use an electronic tire gauge and compare the reading to the inflation level recommended for your tires (you'll find this on a decal on the inside of the driver's door). If your tires are underinflated, you can top them off at a gas station. You'll also need to check the tread of your tires, which you can do by inserting a coin. If you can see all of the head side, you know it's time to get new tires.

OIL

When there's too little oil in your engine, it can fail; when there's too much, it can overheat ... and then fail. This makes checking and maintaining your oil levels crucial, and the good news is, it's an easy job. All you'll need is your car's manual (to show you where to find the dipstick) and a rag. Take the dipstick out of the oil well, clean it with the rag, and dip it into the oil. Remove it again, and check it to see how far up the oil comes. There will be two lines on the dipstick, and your oil level should be between them. Get into the habit of checking your oil levels every time you get gas. This isn't the end of the story with oil, though—you'll also need to change it. Engine oil becomes contaminated over time, and this can affect your engine performance. An oil change will need to be done by a mechanic approximately every six months (your car's manual will tell you exactly how often).

WARNING LIGHTS

It's important to understand the warning lights on your dashboard, as these will alert you to potential issues. The check engine light will come on when there's something going on with your car's emissions, and if this happens, you should visit a mechanic. They'll be able to tell you what caused the light to come on and fix the problem. However, there are times that this light will come on if the gas cap isn't replaced tightly enough—try screwing it on more tightly, and see if the light goes off.

Your oil light is another one to keep an eye on. Depending on your car, you may have a change oil light and an oil warning light. The change oil light does exactly what it says—it tells you it's time to change the oil, but it's not an emergency. The oil warning light, however, tells you that the oil pressure has dipped, and this means it could damage the engine if the oil is not topped up. If, when you check the oil, you discover that the levels are fine, take your car to a me-chanic to find out what the problem is and fix it.

The final warning light to be aware of is the coolant warning light. The coolant helps the car maintain an even temperature, and if the light comes on, it means your car is overheating. If this is left unattended, it could cause serious (and expensive!) issues. If the light comes on while you're driving, pull over and allow the car to cool down. Once it has, drive to the closest gas station you can find and add coolant.

WIPER BLADES AND FLUIDS

Visibility is crucial to your safety, and in order to ensure you have it, you'll need to keep on top of your wiper fluid levels. Your car has a reservoir to hold wiper fluid—just see if it looks low and top it up when it does. You'll only need to do this every few months since you won't be using it constant-ly, and low levels can't damage your engine. You should only wash your windows when you're parked or stopped in traffic if you use it while you're driving, it can obscure your vision and make it dangerous.

The other half of the equation is your wiper blades. These are made of rubber, and that means that, over time, they'll wear out ... and what that means is a streaky windscreen. Check your blades frequently, and if you're a frequent driver, aim to replace them every year.

LIGHTS

Your headlights and taillights are your main form of communication with other drivers, and they're your means of seeing in the dark or in bad weather. This means you'll need to check them regularly to make sure they're in working order. The easiest way to do this is to have a friend or family member help you by watching the lights from the outside while you test them. If they tell you a light is out or too dim, you'll need to replace the bulb as soon as you can.

BRAKES

The majority of cars have disc brakes, which wear out over time. If you hear a squeaking sound when you apply your brakes, this is a clue that your brakes should be serviced. You should also have your brake pads checked by a mechanic every time you have your oil changed, and change them on their recommendation.

BATTERY

Slow engine starts are a sign that your battery may be near the end of its life, and this is a warning worth listening to, as a dead battery could leave you stranded. You can prolong your battery life by avoiding using your headlights, interior lights, or radio when the engine isn't running. Newer batteries come with a sticker that tells you when they were made. If you have to buy a new battery, check the date first to make sure that it's fresh.

emergencies

Keep an emergency kit in your car. You can buy these pre- made, and they contain things like a first aid kit, an emergency blanket, jumper cables, roadside flares, a tool kit, and a flashlight. This will help you if you break down far away from home. It's a good idea to join a roadside emergency service like AAA. While this is an extra monthly cost, in my opinion (and probably your parents' too!), it's a worthwhile investment.

THE ART OF NAVIGATION

I know what you're thinking: Why do I need to know anything about navigation when we have GPS? Well, if you've ever had a pizza delivered to your house by accident, or you've been a passenger in a car that's ended up on a random industrial estate instead of at the sports center, then you'll know that GPS doesn't always have your back. And that means it's important to know how to get by if it goes wrong.

Start by familiarizing yourself with major roadways in your area. Knowing the main roads will help you find your way if you get lost on a minor road. Learn about suburbs, landmarks, and notable buildings for better orientation. Avoid using the same route every time (this will give you backup options in case of road closures). As you explore different routes, your brain will make connections, leading to a thorough understanding of local roads and their connections.

To navigate effectively, try the timeless method of using the sun's position (remembering that it rises in the east and sets in the west) to determine your direction. Physical maps remain valuable, but practice is needed to use them proficiently. Printing a map from Google Maps allows for precise route planning; you can even print out directions. I find it helpful to count the number of roads I'll pass before I have to turn too.

Before you set out, make sure you know roughly how long it should take you to get to your destination. If your journey was only meant to be 15 miles and you still haven't found it after an hour, you've probably made a mistake somewhere along the line. Try to pay attention to landmarks as you're driving—this will make it easier to find your way back if you make a wrong turn. Never be afraid to ask for directions, but only do this if you feel safe. If there's no one around or you feel uncomfortable pulling up alongside someone, drive to a gas station or a shop, and ask in there.

It's essential to know all these backup methods so that you don't have to rely on your sat nav, but it's still a useful piece of technology, and understanding it is important too. You can use something like Google Maps on your phone, or you can use the sat nav built into your car. If you don't have one, you could also consider investing in a third-party unit from a company like TomTom or Garmin.

DRIVING IN OTHER COUNTRIES

When you're studying for your driving test, you'll learn about the rules of the road for the country you live in, but these aren't always the same in other countries. If you'll be driving abroad, make sure you know the rules for the country you'll be driving in, as well as the different road signs and road markings. You'll also need to check that your license is valid in that country and whether your visa will allow you to drive.

In some countries, you drive on the right-hand side of the road, but in others, you drive on the left. This can be confusing if it's the other way around to what you're used to, so try to start in a quiet area and work your way up to bigger roads. Practice making left and right turns before you get to a busy area. In most countries, the driver's seat is on the opposite side of the car from the side of the road you'll be driving on. So if you're in the UK, where they drive on the left, the driver's seat is on the right; if you're in the US, where they drive on the right, the driver's seat is on the left. If you can, try to be a passenger before you drive abroad for the first time—that way, you can get a feel of the vehicle being the other way around and spend some time getting to know the rules without the responsibility.

SAFETY BEHIND THE WHEEL

We have a whole chapter on safety coming up, but driving safety is unique, and I think it's better to include it here. Some of it may seem like common sense, but you'd be surprised by how many experienced drivers still mess up on some of these points.

- Don't use your phone while you're driving unless you're using a hands-free setting.

- If you're getting into your car in a parking lot or on the street, have your keys in your hand so you can get in straight away. Be aware of what's going on around you, lock your doors, and leave as quickly as possible.

- Always wear a seatbelt (regardless of whether you're the driver or a passenger).

- Keep cash in your glove compartment in case you need to get gas or pay for parking in an emergency. Avoid distractions when you're driving. Set your music or GPS destination up before you leave, and avoid eating, drinking, or rooting about for dropped items once you're on the move.

- Keep a charger in your car in case your phone runs out of battery.

- Make sure you have the details of your roadside recovery provider with you so you know exactly who to call in an emergency.

- Park in well-lit areas at night, ideally somewhere with a lot of people around, avoiding spaces where you could get blocked in.

- Fill up with gas during the daylight hours if possible. If you ever feel like someone's following you to your car, change direction and head toward other people. If you're ever uncomfortable with walking to your car, don't be afraid to ask someone to accompany you.

- If you ever feel like someone's following you while you're driving, stay calm. Call the police, and drive toward the nearest police station. It might be tempting to speed in these circumstances, but this won't help you lose them. Your best bet is to head to somewhere they definitely don't want to follow you.

- If you're pulled over by an unmarked car, call the police to check that the person in the car is really a police officer.

- Scan intersections carefully before crossing them.

- Never drive if you're very tired, if you've been drinking, or after using strong medication that causes drowsiness.

It's quite likely that you'll learn to drive when you're still at home and have your parents around to help you out. Ask them as many questions as you can—they've probably been driving a long time, and their experience is valuable. In the next chapter, we'll move on to preparing for the time that you eventually move out and can't rely on your parents as much. That starts with knowing how to keep your home running smoothly. Before we get there, though, it's time for that all-important affirmation:

I have a fantastic new vehicle that fits all my needs perfectly.

8
BEHIND THE SCENES OF SAFE AND COMFORTABLE HOME

In a poll organized by the C.S. Mott Children's Hospital in Michigan, 25% of the parents surveyed admitted that they're the main reason their children aren't more independent. Nowhere is this clearer than in the running of the home. Most teenagers have some chores to do around the house, but do you really know everything that's involved in running a household? I certainly didn't when I first set out on my own—and let me tell you, it was a rude awakening! Let's go through the basics and make sure you don't have to learn the hard way.

FINDING YOUR PLACE TO LIVE

You can't manage a house until you have one, so the first thing to do is find somewhere to live. Perhaps this will be a room in a college dorm; perhaps it will be an apartment, or maybe it will be a small house. The best way to figure out what's right for you is to come up with a budget before you do anything else. In all likelihood, your first home will be rented. Very few young people are in a position to buy as soon as they move away from home. That means your income will need to cover your rent, as well as all your bills and necessities. To get an idea of your budget, add up all your income, and then deduct the cost of all your non-negotiable expenses—that's your rent, utilities, transportation costs, and any annual bills like car insurance. The figure you end up with is what you'll have left for groceries, entertainment, and unexpected expenses. If you don't have enough left for all of that, you'll need to look for cheaper housing. Do this for different rental properties until you figure out what you can afford.

When you're ready to pick somewhere, you'll need to apply to rent it. If your application is successful, you'll have to undergo some background checks and then sign a tenancy agreement, which will tell you how long the contract is for and what rules you must abide by while you live there. You'll be able to pick up the keys on the date that your tenancy begins, and then you'll need to contact the utility suppliers to let them know you'll be taking over all the bills. Your landlord will give you the relevant information and contact numbers when you take over the tenancy.

BASIC HOUSEHOLD TASKS

Once you're in your new place, it's your responsibility to keep everything running smoothly. It might seem a bit daunting to begin with because it will involve things you're not used to dealing with—but it will soon become automatic, and you won't have to worry about it. We're going to look more closely at cleaning in a moment, but if I could give you only one piece of advice, it would be this: Come up with a routine. Once cleaning becomes a habit, it won't be something you neglect, nor will it be something you have to think about.

Offer to help your parents with some of the household tasks even the ones you don't usually do. That way, when it comes time for you to leave home, you'll already know how to do everything, and if there's anything you're not sure about, you can ask your parents as you learn. They're going to love having the extra help and will surely be on board. Help out with each of the following tasks to grow your repertoire:

- doing the dishes—both by hand and in the dishwasher

- taking out the trash and recycling

- cleaning the bathroom

- vacuuming

- making your bed

- dusting surfaces

- tidying clutter

- organizing closets and drawers

- filing paperwork

Ask your parents if there's anything else they think you should learn—I'm sure they'll jump at the chance to help you out!

LAUNDRY

There's no escaping laundry, and since you enjoy wearing well-kept clothes, developing this habit is a win for life. Ask your parents if they'd like your help, and take the opportunity to learn the ropes—you'll make it far easier on yourself later on. Here's what you should know:

- Sort clothes properly. Separate your laundry into different piles based on color and fabric type to prevent color bleeding and damage.

- Follow care labels. Check the care labels on your clothes for specific washing instructions, including water temperature, wash cycle, and drying recommendations.

- Measure the amount of detergent. Do not use excessive amounts since it may leave residue on your clothing. Follow the recommended dosage for your specific load size.

- Treat stains promptly. Address stains before washing by using appropriate stain removers or spot-treating with detergent. This increases the chances of successful stain removal.

- Properly load the washing machine. Avoid overloading the machine, as it can hinder proper cleaning and rinsing. Leave enough space for clothes to move freely.

- Choose appropriate wash cycles. Select the appropriate wash cycle based on the fabric and level of dirtiness. Delicate fabrics may require a gentle or hand wash cycle, while heavily soiled items might need a more intensive cycle.

- Dry clothes properly. Check garment labels for drying instructions. Some items may need to be air- dried, while others can be tumble dried. Avoid excessive heat to prevent shrinking or damaging clothes.

- Fold and store clothes neatly. Once dry, fold or hang clothes promptly to minimize wrinkles and keep your wardrobe organized.

Other things you might want to ask your parents how to do:

- how to use a laundromat

- how to hand wash delicate items

- how to hang clothes up to dry

- how to iron clothing

- how to repair hems and tears and sew on a button

CLEANING A KITCHEN

There's a lot more to keeping a kitchen clean than doing the dishes and emptying the trash. I've split the essential tasks into three lists: daily, weekly, and monthly jobs. You can use these as checklists once you're out on your own, and if there's anything you're not sure how to do, ask your parents to show you.

DAILY TASKS

- Wash dishes. Some items—like wooden utensils or cast iron dishes—can't go in the dishwasher, so pay attention to how your family does it.

- Clean the sink (this is particularly important if you've been washing anything that's come into contact with raw meat).

- Wipe down the stove, work surfaces, and small appliances.

- Put away anything left out on the work surfaces. Take out the trash and replace the trash bag.

- Sweep the entire floor (including under the table and in the corners).

WEEKLY TASKS

- Mop the kitchen floor.

- Clean the inside of the microwave.

- Clean the outside of the kitchen cupboards and fridge/freezer.

MONTHLY TASKS

- Clean the oven. You might think that once a month is unnecessary for this job, but trust me, it's worth it. You don't want to clean an oven with six months' worth of baked-on grease in it. Take it from someone who once had to resort to using a wallpaper scraper!

- Clean the inside of the fridge (and throw away out- of-date items).

CLEANING A BATHROOM

Next up is the bathroom. My least favorite job, but let's face it—it has to be done. Personally, I like to keep on top of it by cleaning the toilet and the sink at the end of every day, but for some people, doing the whole bath-room once a week is enough. Follow these tips to keep on top of grime and bacteria.

Toilet

It's not just the bowl you need to think about here—it's important to make sure the handle and seat are germ-free too. To cover all bases, follow these steps:

- Add toilet cleaner to the bowl, and allow it to sit for 5 minutes before scrubbing with a toilet brush and flushing.

- Wipe the handle and toilet seat with a disinfectant spray or wipes.

- Spray the toilet brush with disinfectant after each use.

Sink

The sink is another place where germs can easily build up. Following these steps will help you keep on top of it:

- Spray the sink with a disinfectant spray or bathroom cleaner, wipe with a cloth, and rinse with warm water.

- Wipe the faucet handles with a cloth and disinfectant spray or wipes

Bathtub

You can help yourself out here by rinsing the tub after every use, but it should still get a more thorough cleaning every week. Here's what to do:

- Spray the shower and tub with a bathroom cleaner or disinfectant spray, and wipe down with a cloth and warm water.

- When the grime is tougher, use a sponge with a foam cleanser designed to cut through soap scum.

Tile Grout

You've probably encountered bathrooms where the grout is discolored and (let's be honest) a bit grim looking. You can avoid this by following this plan once a week:

- Mix ¾ cup of bleach with 1 gallon of water.

- Wear rubber gloves, and use a brush to apply your mixture to one area at a time. Allow this to sit for a few minutes, scrub the area, and then rinse it.

Floor

You might not notice the dirt on your bathroom floor, but trust me; it's there. Clean it once a week by vacuuming or sweeping up the dust and hair and then mopping it with a solution of hot water and disinfectant. You can speed up the drying process by turning on the fan.

Fan

Many people overlook the fan, but do this for long enough, and you'll quickly find that it becomes less efficient. Vacuum the dust away, and clean the fan with disinfectant. If you can remove the grill, you can soak it in warm, soapy water for a more thorough clean—just don't forget to dry it before you replace it.

CLEANING YOUR LIVING SPACES

Do yourself a favor, and take the stress out of having guests over—keep your living areas clean the whole time instead of rushing around like a lunatic an hour before your friends are due over. Here's an easy formula to follow:

- Tidy up and put everything away before you begin cleaning.

- Dust hard-to-reach places with a feather duster, beginning with the places highest up so that you don't spread dust to spots you've already cleaned. Use a damp microfiber cloth on surfaces, door handles, and picture frames.

- Clean the TV screen with a dry microfiber cloth, wiping it up and down rather than in circular motions. Don't spray cleaning products or water directly onto the screen.

- If you have wooden furniture, use a furniture polish to protect the wood.

- Clean windows and mirrors using a glass cleaning spray or a solution of equal parts white vinegar and hot water, and a drop of liquid soap. Scrunch up some old newspaper (yes, really!), and rub it in circular motions over the glass until it comes up streak-free.

- Vacuum curtains and blinds, as well as armchairs, couches, and any other soft furnishings you have.

- Vacuum carpets and rugs in the same direction to avoid strange patterns, and use the attachments to reach under furniture. Remember to remove rugs so you can vacuum the carpet underneath them—you'd be amazed by how dirty it can get under there!

- If you have a hard floor, vacuum it first and then mop it. Let it dry completely before putting any rugs back down.

CLEANING A BEDROOM

You've been tidying your bedroom for years, but do you really know what it takes to properly clean it? Follow these steps to make sure you cover everything:

- Make your bed. Aim to change your sheets once a week, washing and drying the old ones immediately so that they're ready the next time you need them.

- Organize any clothes lying around. If you're not sure whether it's clean or dirty, play it safe and class it as dirty.

- Return anything that you've left out to its storage space.

- Dust all the surfaces with a duster, again, starting with the highest places and working your way down. Wipe down any surfaces that are sticky with a damp cloth.

- Vacuum the floor and soft furnishings (apart from the bed), following the advice we looked at in the living room section.

- Clean the mirrors and windows, using the same approach you took with the living room.

HOME MAINTENANCE AND MINOR REPAIR TASKS

First things first: There are some home repair tasks you shouldn't attempt to carry out yourself, and any task you're not sure how to do, you should ask for help with. It's always ok to contact your landlord or call out a handyperson, and in the case of the following tasks, it's mandatory:

- electrical rewiring removing mold

- major plumbing work

- structural modifications

- pest infestations

- water damage

Now let's take a look at the things you can do yourself.

- **Turn off the Water Supply:** The water supply for your home is controlled by a main water valve, and it's important to know where it is. Common places to find this valve are on a wall outside, in the basement or garage, or in a utility room. If you ever have a burst pipe or a leak, you might need to shut off the water. Some have lever handles; others have wheel ones. If you have the wheel type, you'll need to turn it clockwise if you need to turn the water off, and if you have the lever type, you'll need to turn it a quarter turn so that it lies parallel with the water pipe.

- **Hang a Picture:** If you want to hang something heavy, your first task is to find a wall stud (these are the vertical boards holding the walls up). You can find this by knocking on the wall—you'll know when you hit one because the sound will change. This part of the wall is more secure, and your picture is more likely to stay up. Hammer a nail in securely, and hang your picture.

- **Unblock a Sink:** You can do this by using a plunger. If the water isn't draining away properly, cover the plughole with the plunger, and pump it until the blockage clears. If it still isn't draining properly, you can buy clog removal chemicals, which you pour down the plug and leave to work their magic—just follow the directions on the bottle.

- **Fill a Hole in a Wall:** If you have small holes from screws or nails, you can fill them easily with spackle. Level it out so that it's flat, and when it's dry, sand it down until it's smooth. Then paint over it with paint that matches the color of the wall.

- **Fix a Squeaking Door:** Whether it's a cupboard door or the door to your living room, a spray of WD-40 on the hinges will loosen things up and stop it from squeaking. If you don't have any, a smear of petroleum jelly will work in a pinch.

- **Recaulk a Sink or Bathtub:** If any of the caulking comes away, you can fix it yourself, and this is a good idea because it will stop water damage from occurring. Remove the damaged area with a sharp knife, and tape a border around the area you're going to caulk to give you lines to work within. You can buy a caulk gun and some caulk from a hardware store. Cut the tube of caulk at a 45° angle, bearing in mind that you'll get a smaller line of caulk if you cut closer to the end of the tube. Load the caulk gun with the tube and carefully apply the contents to the area. Smooth it out, and allow it to dry before you use the sink again.

- **Clean Your Washer/Dryer:** Front-load washers tend to gather mold, and you can deal with this by setting the machine to its hottest cleaning cycle and adding two cups of vinegar with a quarter of a cup of baking soda. Allow the cycle to finish, and then wipe the drum and seal with a sponge. For the dryer, you should clean the vent after every load and empty the duct. You can do this by unplugging the machine and vacuuming away the lint.

- **Clean Your Garbage Disposal:** If your sink starts to smell, pour baking soda and vinegar down either side of the garbage disposal. The mixture will foam and break up the dirt. Leave it for a few minutes, and then run the hot water to wash it away.

- **Reset a Tripped Switch:** If you have a lot of electrical appliances running at the same time, sometimes the circuit breaker will trip, and everything will stop working. This can be alarming the first time it happens, but it's easy to fix. Open your circuit box, and look at the switches. You'll be able to see which one has tripped because it will be set to "Off." Flip it back to the "On" position, and your appliances should function normally.

No matter how prepared you are, there will always be repair jobs that take you by surprise. Remember, you can always look things up online—and if in doubt, contact your landlord or a handyperson.

You might have noticed the obvious part of running a household that's missing from this chapter—grocery shopping and cooking. That's because this topic deserves a chapter all of its very own, and that's what's coming up next. Not before an affirmation, though (I hope you're repeating these to yourself regularly and feeling yourself growing in confidence!)

I live in a harmonious place, I am safe, and everything is well.

9

KITCHEN MASTERY AND SHOPPING SAVVINESS

My friend's daughter loves cooking. He's always encouraged her, but recently, he had an eye-opening realization. He understood that he hadn't been letting her explore recipes and shop for ingredients independently. "She's a great cook," he said, "But unless I let her take charge, she's not going to be prepared to put her skills to good use when she lives on her own." It was a good point and links back to what we discussed about healthy living in Chapter One—being able to shop for and cook healthy and delicious meals is essential. Let's walk through the whole process.

A HEALTHY SHOPPING LIST

The key to a successful grocery shop is planning for every meal of each day before you go to the store. Follow these steps, and you'll be well on your way:

- Check what you already have in your fridge and food cupboards, and think about how you could use it for meals.

- Plan a couple of meals with the ingredients you already have.

- Plan the rest of the meals for the week, including any side dishes and drinks.

- Find recipes for any meal you don't already know how to make.

- Make a list of the ingredients you'll need to buy.

Your meal plan will tell you what you need on your shopping list, and if you've been thorough, you'll have all your snacks accounted for too. But the best-laid plans sometimes go awry, so it's a good idea to know how to make a healthy shopping list without a meal plan. Organize your list by areas of the store, and follow these tips (including items from every food group) to make grocery shopping a breeze:

Produce: Look for a variety of fruits and vegetables spanning a range of colors. Try to buy produce that's both locally grown and seasonal—this is both cheaper and better for the environment.

Dairy and Eggs: Look for low-fat dairy products. If you like whole-fat cheese, opt for strong cheeses so that you get a lot of flavor in a smaller amount. Avoid flavored yogurts because they have a lot of sugar in them. And here's a secret—you can make far tastier yogurt by buying it plain and adding your own fruit or a teaspoon of jam.

Meat and Seafood: Try to eat fish twice a week, and if you eat red meat, opt for leaner cuts. For lower-fat options, choose chicken and turkey over red meat.

Bakery: Look for bread that lists whole wheat flour at the top of its ingredients list. Choose bread with 3-4 grams of fiber per slice.

Rice and Pasta: Choose whole grains like whole wheat spaghetti and brown rice.

Sauces and Condiments: These can be very high in sugar and salt, so choose sugar-free varieties where you can. High-fat condiments like mayonnaise can be replaced with lighter versions.

Breakfast Cereals: Go for whole-grain, unsweetened cereals like oatmeal or muesli. You can always add dried fruit and nuts to liven them up a bit.

Canned Foods: Choose low-salt soups and fish and legumes canned in water rather than oil or brine. If you're buying canned fruit, choose those that are canned in fruit juice rather than syrup. And a word to the wise—it's worth having a few cans of diced tomatoes in your cart. You can always whip up a meal if you have those on hand.

Frozen Food: If you have freezer space, it's a good idea to buy frozen fruit and vegetables. That way, you'll always have them available to add to a meal, even if you haven't had a chance to stock up on fresh varieties. Try to avoid pre-packaged meals, and if you do choose convenience foods like pizza or waffles, choose whole grain, low-sodium versions.

Snacks: Stock up on healthy snacks so you're not tempted to make Homer Simpson-style food choices if hunger strikes. Dried fruit, nuts, seeds, whole grain crackers, and dark chocolate are good choices.

Drinks: Water is the healthiest thing you can drink, but if you're not a fan, try buying sparkling water, unsweetened teas, and fruit juice. (Make sure it really is juice though—if it's labeled as a "juice drink," it's going to be packed with sugar.)

PICKING PRODUCE WELL

With the basics of the shopping list covered, it's time to delve a little deeper. You know what to shop for, but how can you make sure you're choosing the best options? Produce is where this matters the most, and it took me ages to figure out the secrets. I want to save you the pain of avocados you can't do anything with for weeks and cucumbers that go mushy within days. Before we get down to specifics, use these three rules to guide you:

Don't be fooled by perfect-looking produce. Just because it's symmetrical and glistening, it doesn't mean it's the best apple. The most delicious fruits and vegetables often have irregular shapes and imperfections.

Use your hands. You'll get a better idea of the quality of the produce by picking it up. Signs of freshness are taught skin or peel and a heavy fruit or vegetable.

Be guided by the seasons. Just because you can buy tomatoes all year round, it doesn't mean you should. When they're in season, they'll taste better, have better nutrient density, and be better for your bank balance.

With that as your baseline, here's what to look out for when you're shopping for the perfect produce:

- **Apples:** They should be firm and heavy with smooth skin and no bruising. The smaller it is, the more flavor it will have.

- **Avocados:** Look for those that are dent-free with taut skin. It should give a little under pressure—it shouldn't be hard.

- **Bananas:** Look for uniformly yellow skin. Small brown spots show that they're at their sweetest. Watch out for bruises or split skins.

- **Bell peppers:** These should be firm and heavy with bright, wrinkle-free skin. Stems should be bright green.

- **Blueberries:** These should be firm and plump. Don't forget to check for crushed or rotten berries at the bottom of the container.

- **Broccoli:** This vegetable should have rigid stems and tight floret clusters deep green or purplish in color. Avoid yellowing heads, as these may be bitter.

- **Carrots:** Search out carrots that are firm, smooth, and bright orange in color. Avoid bendy carrots or those with cracked bases. The freshest ones will have bright green leaves.

- **Cauliflower:** Look for firm, bright leaves with no spots on the florets. Cauliflowers should be ivory white with tight florets.

- **Cucumber:** It is important to find cucumbers that are firm and uniformly dark green, with no yellow blemishes, softness, or wrinkles.

- **Eggplant:** These should be heavy with smooth, shiny skin and a green stem. Avoid eggplants that are shriveled, soft, or have spots. The flesh should bounce back when you press gently.

- **Garlic:** Cloves should be tightly closed and remain firm when you press them. Avoid shriveled or damp bulbs with spots.

- **Grapefruit:** Seek out fruit that is heavy with skin that gives a little when pressed. Imperfections in skin and color won't affect the flavor.

- **Grapes:** Go for grapes that are plump, firmly attached to the stem, and without wrinkles. Look for red grapes without a green tinge and green grapes with a slight yellowness. The presence of a silvery- white powder means they should stay fresher for longer.

- **Green Beans:** These should be bright and smooth with no sign of withering. If you bend them gently, they should snap.

- **Kale:** Look for moist, dark blue-green leaves with no sign of wilting or discoloration. Kale with smaller leaves will be more tender.

- **Kiwi:** The best fruit will be firm but will give a little under pressure. Avoid fruit that's bruised, wrinkled, or mushy.

- **Leeks:** Smaller leeks are best—larger ones may be tough and woody. Look for green tops and blemishless root ends, and avoid those with yellowing or spotted leaves.

- **Lemons and Limes:** Heavy fruit that is fragrant and brightly colored with thin, smooth skin is ideal. Small brown splotches are ok, but the fruit will spoil quicker, so use it quickly. Avoid lemons with a green tinge.

- **Lettuce (Iceberg):** Firm, solid heads with clean outer leaves and tight inside leaves are best.

- **Lettuce (Romaine):** Look for crisp leaves with no rust spots or browning edges. Inside leaves should be paler.

- **Mango:** This should be firm but will give a little when squeezed. Check to see if it is fragrant by the stem.

- **Melon (Cantaloupe):** A slight oval shape with a smooth indentation by the stem is good. The opposite end should give a little when pressed. Avoid melons with soft spots.

- **Melon (Watermelon):** Find a melon that is firm, heavy, and free of cuts or dents. The skin should be dull with a creamy underside. If you tap it, you should hear a hollow thump.

- **Mushrooms:** Look for firm, closed caps. Avoid slimy mushrooms or those with soft dark spots. If the gills are visible, they should be eaten sooner rather than later.

- **Onions:** Try to find onions with dry, crisp outer skin with no soft spots, dark blemishes, or without signs of sprouting.

- **Potatoes:** Look for smooth skin with no cracks, bruises, or green tinges. You'll probably find better quality potatoes if you buy them loose.

- **Tomatoes:** These should have firm flesh with shiny, brightly colored skin. Avoid those with blemishes or spots.

- **Zucchini:** Hunt for those that are heavy and firm with no soft spots. Look for smaller zucchinis (these have more flavor) that are deep green in color.

THE RIGHT MEAT FOR THE RIGHT MEAL

Remember my whole-chicken disaster? That's what you want to avoid, and when you're faced with an aisle full of different meat cuts, if you don't know which kind you need, it's all too easy to come away with the wrong thing. Let's start there and then move on to how you can make sure you're choosing high-quality meat.

Beef: This comes from cows and is high in protein and iron. It's available ground, diced, in strips, or as steaks or roasting joints. If you're making burgers or pasta sauces, you want ground beef; for making stews or kebabs, you want it diced; for stir-fries, you want strips. You'll find a variety of fat levels in most cases—lean beef contains less fat.

Lamb: Lamb can be found diced or ground or in the form of chops, steaks, or roasting joints. Diced meat works well in stews and curries, and ground meat is used in a variety of Asian dishes or traditional English dishes like shepherd's pie.

Pork: From pigs, pork is versatile and comes ground, diced, as chops, steaks, strips, and roasting joints. It can be used ground or diced in many Asian dishes and can be used as a substitute for beef in stews and chilis.

Chicken/Turkey: These meats are low in fat and high in protein. They come in legs, thighs, wings, and breasts, as well as diced, ground, or as the whole bird. Diced meat can be used for pie fillings or stir- fries, while ground meat makes a healthy substitute for ground beef in pasta sauces or burgers. Chicken breast is a leaner, drier cut, while fattier cuts like the legs and thighs are flavor-rich and work well in stews or tray bakes.

CHOOSING MEAT WELL

There's more to buying meat than just taking the first packet you see off the shelf. The first thing to look for is the color, which should be consistent throughout the cut—no area should be darker or lighter than the rest. Pork, lamb, and beef have marbling (streaks of fat), which adds flavor, so don't be put off by white stripes. Pay attention to the smell, too—if it smells rancid, steer clear. The last thing to look for is the firmness of the meat. It should feel firm but not hard, and it should give a little if you push it. If you can push through the cut, it's too soft and means it's passed its best.

Let's go back to those main meat types so you can see exactly what you're looking for in each:

Beef: Look for bright red colors—these indicate quality and freshness. Press it lightly. If it feels soft, it's probably not good. You're looking for a firm texture that bounces back when you push it.

Lamb: Look for pinkish-brown meat with creamy white fat. If it's gray or very bloody with yellow fat, avoid it. The meat should be firm but not tough.

Pork: Look for meat that's somewhere between pale pink and white, with clear marbling. It should be firm and moist-looking without being slimy.

Chicken/turkey: Look for pale-colored meat with a smooth texture and no signs of bruising or discoloration. It should be plump and firm.

TOP TIPS FOR GROCERY SHOPPING

You have your meal plan, you have your shopping list, and you know how to pick good quality produce and meat. Follow these tips to level up your grocery shopping game even further:

- If you struggle with shopping lists, try a shopping app. AnyList is a good one, or you could try Out of Milk or Smart Shopping List.

- Don't go shopping if you're hungry. (This is when unhealthy impulse buying happens ... cue the donut hangover!)

- Check use-by-dates, and if there's a choice, always pick the items with the longest dates.

- Visit the fridge and freezer aisles last to avoid warm cheese and melted ice cream.

- Keep a cooler in your car for transporting frozen items.

- Shop in the evening—you can often find great reductions at the end of the day.

- If you have freezer space, consider buying in bulk to save money.

- Compare the prices of different brands, and look carefully at unit prices—sometimes buying a bigger box is better value than buying a smaller one.

- Look at all the shelves. Grocery stores are crafty, and they'll often put the most expensive products at eye level. Cheaper brands are often kept on the top or bottom shelf.

- Look out for money-saving coupons in the mail, online, or in local newspapers.

- Join the loyalty program—you can often get discounts and rewards this way. Bear in mind, however, that loyalty programs are different from membership cards—the latter are paid memberships, whereas the former are usually free.

- Read the nutritional information on labels, and avoid products with excessive added ingredients.

- Use the calculator on your phone to keep track of how much you're spending as you go around the store.

- Always use a cart or a basket, even if you only need a few things. (All it takes is having to compare two products, and suddenly you don't have enough hands!)

- Stay around the edges of the store to find the freshest products and minimize your risk of buying junk food.

ESSENTIAL COOKING SKILLS

There are so many kitchen skills to learn, and you're going to spend a life-time acquiring them. But there are a few that you'll need as a foundation to build on, so let's make sure we have those. I've divided them into general skills, which you'll need no matter what you're cooking, and specific skills, which have to do with particular meals.

GENERAL SKILLS

Safety Basics: Wash your hands and clean your surfaces often. Keep eggs, seafood, raw meat, and poultry away from food that's ready to eat. Avoid leaving food out at room temperature for over two hours. Refrigerate it as soon as it has cooled down.

Knife Skills: All knife skills take practice, but here are the basics of what you need to know.

- **Chopping:** Hold the handle with your middle, ring, and little fingers, and hold the blade between your index finger and thumb. Keep the handle-end of the blade near the chopping board, and point the tip upwards as you chop.

- **Mincing:** This is a similar technique to chopping. Cut your ingredients into strips, turn them 90 degrees, and cut them again, anchoring the tip of the blade on the chopping board. Work quickly for best results.

- **Dicing:** This method is for cutting fruit and vegetables into cubes. Start by cutting the food into equal square-sided pieces. Then line them up, and cut everything into cubes.

- **Chiffonade:** This is for cutting salad leaves and herbs. Remove the stems, pile the leaves up with the smallest ones at the top, and rock the knife forwards and backward over them.

- **Batonnet:** Use this method for making vegetable sticks for dipping. Chop the ends off your vegetables, and then square off the sides to make a rectangle.Slice this into pieces, pile them up, and cut them again.

Seasoning: For best results, season your food as you're cooking it, sprinkling salt from a height to make sure it distributes evenly.

SPECIFIC SKILLS

Boiling an egg: Start with the egg at room temperature. For soft-boiled eggs, lower the egg into a pan of boiling water, and boil for 3-5 minutes. For hard-boiled eggs, place your egg into a pan of cold water, and bring it up to a boil before cooking it for 7-10 minutes. To prevent it from overcooking, plunge it into cold water immediately.

PRO TIP: *Use the spin test. Place the egg on a flat surface, and spin it gently. If it spins smoothly and quickly, it's likely hard- boiled. If it wobbles or doesn't spin much, it's still raw or partially cooked.*

Cooking Pasta: To eat pasta the Italian way, you want to cook it al-dente, which means that it's firm to the bite. To do this, fill your pan with enough water to cover double the amount of pasta you're using, add salt, and bring it to a boil. Add the pasta, and cook it for 10-12 minutes, stirring occasionally to prevent it from sticking. Different kinds of pasta have different cooking times, so always read the directions.

PRO TIP: *Adding oil after cooking prevents the pasta from sticking together, but contrary to popular belief, adding oil to the boiling water won't prevent it from sticking. Instead, drizzle a small amount of olive oil over your pasta once you've drained it.*

Toss it gently to coat the strands, which will help to minimize sticking.

Cooking Rice: Use a ratio of 1:1.5 rice to water. Rinse your rice under cold water, and then add to a large pan. Cover it with water, and bring it to a boil over medium heat before placing a lid on the pan and reducing the temperature. Cook for 12-15 minutes or until the rice has absorbed all the water. Fluff it with a fork.

PRO TIP: *After rice is cooked, it retains some residual steam and moisture. Placing a clean kitchen towel or a paper towel over the pot or rice cooker helps absorb this excess moisture. The towel acts as a barrier, preventing condensation from dripping back onto the rice and making it soggy.*

Making an Omelet: Start by heating an omelet pan or nonstick skillet over medium heat. When the pan is heated, add a tiny quantity of butter or oil, making sure it coats the bottom. Beat the eggs with salt, pepper, and any other ingredients in a separate bowl. Pour the mixture into the preheated pan, tilting it to spread the eggs evenly. Let the edges set, gently pushing them toward the center to allow uncooked eggs to flow.

PRO TIP: *If you wish, add fillings to one-half of the omelet. Fold it in half, and cook for another minute until fully set but still moist. Slide onto a plate, and you'll have a deliciously cooked omelet with a flavorful filling.*

Separating an Egg: Use the blunt edge of a knife to crack the shell. Open it so that you have two halves, and then pass the yolk between the two pieces of shell, allowing the white to drop into a bowl. Place the yolk in a separate bowl.

PRO TIP: *Alternatively, crack the egg into a small bowl, then place the opening of an empty plastic water bottle near the yolk as you squeeze it, slowly releasing the squeeze to let the suction pull the yolk into the bottle while leaving the egg white behind.*

Browning Meat: If you're making a stew or a casserole, you want to make sure the meat is juicy and tender. To do this, you'll need to seal it first, which is done by pan-frying it briefly until the outside is brown before adding it to your dish.

PRO TIP: *Ensure that the meat is dry before adding it to a hot pan, as moisture on the surface can hinder browning. Avoid overcrowding the pan, allowing enough space between pieces to ensure proper heat distribution and to avoid steaming instead of browning. Sprinkle some salt at the end to make it even more tender and juicy.*

Roasting Vegetables: This is the most flavorful way to cook vegetables. Cut them into similar-sized pieces to ensure even cooking. Preheat the oven to 190°C/ 350°F, arrange the vegetables in a roasting tin (in one layer), coat them with olive oil, and season with your desired herbs and spices. Put the tray in the oven, stirring the vegetables occasionally.

PRO TIP: *Root vegetables like carrots will take 40-50 minutes; softer vegetables like peppers and squashes will be done in 15-20 minutes, so remove them earlier.*

Baking Potatoes: Prick your potato with a fork, rub olive oil and a little salt on the outside with your hands, and place it directly on the oven rack at about 200°C / 400°F for 1 hour and 20 minutes.

PRO TIP: *Boiling potatoes before baking them helps to cook them partially, ensuring even cooking, improving texture, and infusing them with flavor.*

READING RECIPES

You might wonder why this part gets its own separate subheading—it's just reading, right? Well, not exactly. There's a way to read a recipe to make sure you get the best results. Follow this process.

1. **Read the entire recipe.** No matter how simple it looks, read the whole thing before you do anything. I learned this the hard way. If you don't do this, you easily end up three steps into the process, realizing you need to quickly add a carrot you haven't even chopped yet.

2. **Understand the ingredients.** Usually, the ingredients are listed in the order in which they're needed and are found at the beginning of the recipe. If you see the word "divided" after any ingredient, it means it will be used more than once, so it shouldn't be added in one go.

3. **Pay attention to the measurements.** The author will have tested the measurements that work best, so follow them carefully. If teaspoons and tablespoons are mentioned, use a measuring spoon rather than

what you think is probably a tablespoon from your silverware drawer. Pay attention to the order of the words, too—1 cup of chopped nuts is very different from 1 cup of nuts, chopped. In the first instance, the nuts should be chopped before they're measured; in the second, the nuts should be measured before you chop them.

4. **Get everything you need ready.** Lay out all the ingredients (ideally, already measured) and all the utensils you'll need before you start cooking. This saves you from burning something while you're running around looking for an ingredient you haven't prepared.

5. **Test the dish.** The recipe will give you a cooking time and tell you what the dish should be like when it's ready, but often the cooking time spans a range to account for different kitchens. Test the dish at the beginning of the time range to see if it fits the description of the finished product, and if it doesn't, give it a bit longer.

We've looked a lot at how to live independently over the last two chapters. But everything from finding somewhere to live to healthy grocery shopping requires one important thing: money! We'll look at that in the next chapter, but first, it's time for our affirmation:

I deserve to cook and eat things that are nutritious and delicious.

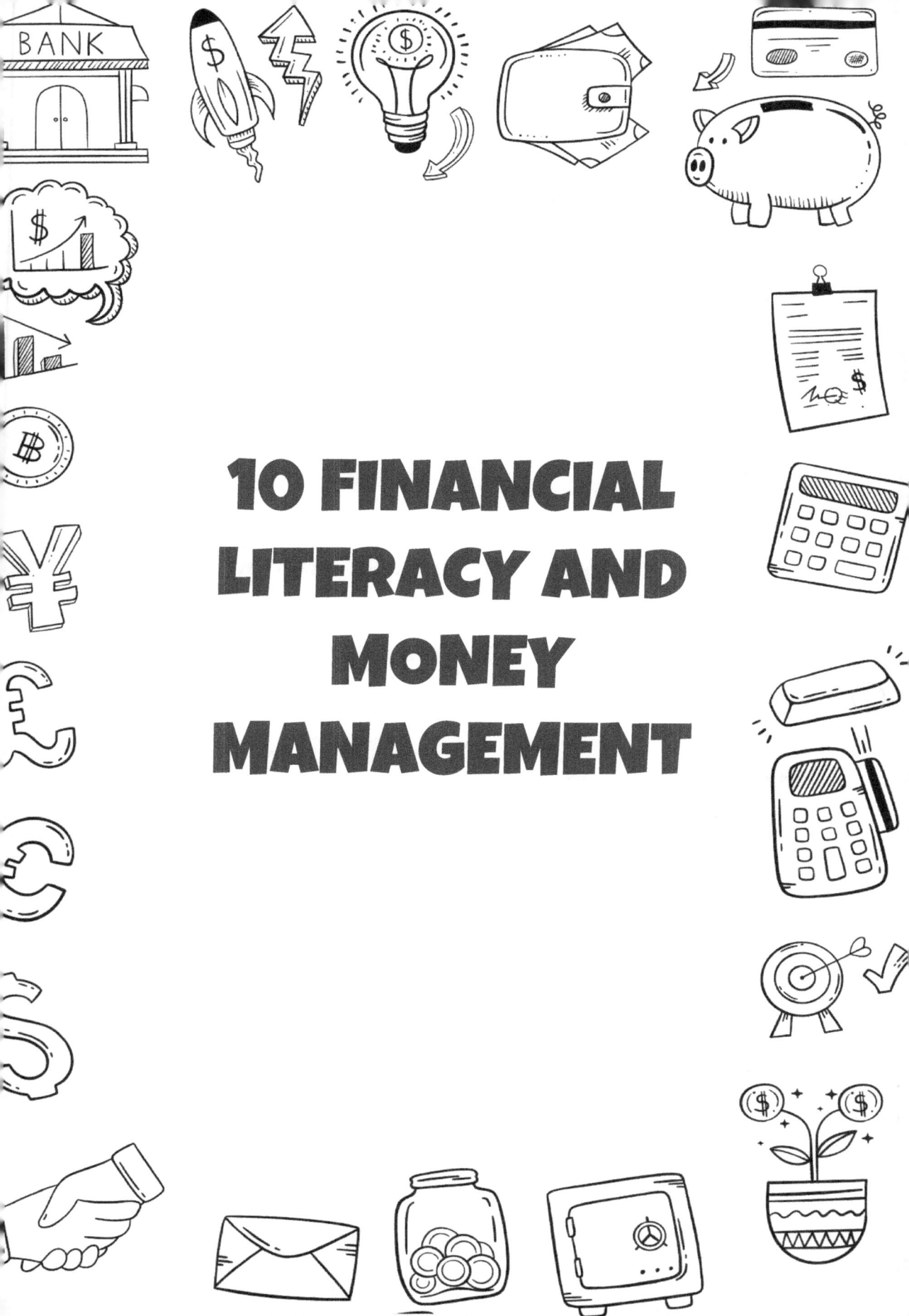

10 FINANCIAL LITERACY AND MONEY MANAGEMENT

Why do you think your parents started giving you pocket money when you were younger? To an extent, it was about giving you independence so you could buy what you wanted, but there was more to it than that. It was also about teaching you how money works and what to do with it. This is a fundamental life skill known as financial literacy, and building on it is important so that you make good decisions, become more independent, and are financially stable—and when life throws financial challenges at you (and trust me, it will!), you'll know how to handle them. Let's dive in.

BANK ACCOUNTS EXPLAINED

Let's start with bank accounts. Your bank account is where you'll keep the money you use to run your life and buy the things you need. It's much safer than keeping all your money as cash, and you'll always have access to it. In the modern world, it's almost impossible not to have one—most financial transactions will require you to use a credit or debit card, use an app like PayPal, write a check, and receive deposits (when you get paid for your work, for example). None of this is possible without a bank account.

DIFFERENT TYPES OF BANKS

We tend to think of buildings when we think of banks, but this isn't always the case. Those that exist within buildings are known as brick-and-mortar banks, and most will allow you to manage your accounts online. Some banks, however, only operate online. These banks offer the same services, but it's not possible to physically go into them.

Most people have accounts with **retail banks**, which are for- profit companies that offer a range of financial services, including checking and savings accounts, credit cards, loans, and insurance. Retail banks are sometimes online only, and sometimes they have brick-and-mortar branches. This is the type of bank that usually has the most ATMs.

The other option is a **credit union**, which offers all the financial products retail banks do. The difference is that they're not-for-profit, and they're owned by their members. They usually have better interest rates and lower fees, but they tend not to have as many branches or ATMs.

DIFFERENT TYPES OF BANK ACCOUNTS

Whatever type of bank you use, it will offer different types of accounts. There are three main ones that most people use.

- **Savings Account:** These are accounts that will earn you some interest, but it's not usually very high. They're reliable and secure, though, and they allow you to access your money easily (although there are often limitations on how often you can take it out), which makes them useful for short-term savings.

- **Checking Account/Current Account:** Different countries name these accounts differently, but they're essentially the same. They allow you to withdraw and deposit money (either at a bank, an ATM, or through electronic transfer), and you can withdraw from them as often as you need. They earn little (if any) interest. Watch out for fees with this type of account. There are often penalties for going into your overdraft or using an ATM not owned by the bank.

- **High-Yield Savings Accounts:** These pay a much higher interest rate than regular savings accounts, but you usually need to make a much bigger initial deposit when you set one up and store much more money in the account to keep it open.

CREDIT CARDS AND DEBIT CARDS

Every adult you know carries plastic cards in their wallet ... but they don't all operate the same way. Here's the difference between the two big payment cards:

- **Debit Cards:** These take money straight out of your checking account, meaning that you can never spend more than you have in your bank.

They don't help you build a credit rating, though. (We'll get to what that means in a moment.)

- **Credit Cards:** There's a joke that makes these tricksy little cards easy to understand: *"Why is spicy food like a credit card?* You pay for it the next day."* Credit cards enable you to borrow money without spending anything in your checking account. They're useful for big or unexpected purchases, but you have to use them carefully. If you don't pay back (in full) everything you borrowed each month, your balance carries forward—and that means you have to pay back interest as well as the original amount. If you pay them back religiously, however, they help you build up a good credit rating, and what that means is that you'll qualify for better credit cards and better interest rates on loans. When you apply for a credit card, pay attention to the APR. This is the annual percentage rate, and it tells you how much interest you'll owe on any balance you carry forward.

TYPES OF CREDIT CARDS

Your credit score will determine what cards are available to you, but it's good to know what's out there. When you've never had one before (or later, if you find yourself with bad credit), you'll most likely need to apply for a subprime or secured credit card. If you pay these back on time, your credit score will go up, and you'll qualify for better rates. Once you have a good credit score, your options open up considerably:

- **Cash-Back Cards:** These offer some of what you borrowed back at the end of every month.

- **Travel Reward Cards:** These offer points that you can use for traveling, often covering flights, rental cars, and hotels.

- **Balance Transfer Cards:** These allow you to transfer the balance from one card to another. That can be useful if you owe money on cards with higher interest rates and want to move them so you can pay them back more quickly.

- **Low-APR Cards:** These cards charge little to no interest and are helpful if you regularly carry your balance forward—they could save you hundreds in interest payments.

CURRENCIES OF THE WORLD

Before we zone in on your money, let's widen our scope a little and look at money in the world at large. You probably know that every country doesn't use the same currency ... but do you know why that is? It's because every country has a unique economy and has to make financial decisions based on its own needs.

Different currencies are worth different amounts: $1 (US dollar), £1 (GB pound), and €1 (European euro) are not worth the same value. You might be able to buy a candy bar in most countries, but if you buy it in the USA, it could cost you a dollar. In Indonesia, it might cost you 14,000 rupiah. That doesn't mean that the candy is more expensive in Indonesia; it means that one dollar is equal to thousands of rupiah. Where it gets complicated, though, is that exchange rates aren't fixed, and they change constantly depending on the global economy. We won't put our Wall Street hats on right now—there are whole books that could be written on currency and why its value changes. Unless you later get into trading it, you don't need to know the ins and outs to get a basic understanding of money. What's good to know at this stage, however, is what the world's most tradable currencies are, simply because these are the ones that affect the market and the ones which you're most likely to encounter. They are as follows:

- US Dollar (USD)
- European Euro (EUR)
- Japanese Yen (JPY)
- British Pound (GBP)
- Swiss Franc (CHF)
- Canadian Dollar (CAD)
- Australian Dollar (AUD)
- New Zealand Dollar (NZD)
- South African Rand (ZAR)

WHERE TO EXCHANGE CURRENCY FOR TRAVELING

When different currencies become most relevant to you is when you're traveling. When you travel overseas, you'll most likely need to exchange currency so that you have the cash to spend in the country where you're traveling. This is worth knowing about in advance because if you rely on hotels and airports, you'll run into high fees and poor exchange rates— in short, you lose out. The best option is to convert your currency before you travel.

Begin by checking what a good exchange rate is for the country you're visiting. This will give you an idea of who's offering you the best deal. The best places to get your money changed are usually:

- local banks and credit unions (These often have the best rates.)

- major international banks (These often have ATMs in different countries.)

- online currency converters like Travelex (Watch out with those—ordering cash online often involves charges for delivery and a worse exchange rate.)

If you don't have time to change your currency before you leave or you'd rather not travel with cash, check to see if your bank has ATMs in your destination country. If so, use an ATM in the airport when you get there rather than using the airport currency exchange kiosk.

MANAGING YOUR MONEY

Knowing how to exchange currency is useful, but you won't be traveling most of the time—you'll be using your money in your country of residence, and managing it well is key.

The foundation for this is knowing how much money you have coming in every month, whether that's from your job, in the form of a loan or a grant, or as an allowance from your parents or guardians. It's also essential to know how much is certain to go out every month—that will be things like your phone bill, rent, utility bills, and grocery shopping. Once you have this clear in your head, you can work with what you have to make sure you're always in control.

THE ART OF BUDGETING

Budgeting allows you to live within your means—meaning that you don't spend more than you have or risk running out of money each month when there are still things left to pay for. It means you can identify when you need to change the way you spend and prepare for unexpected expenses. (Sorry, there's no escaping these!)

There are a few different methods you can use to help you with your budgeting:

- **50/30/20 Rule:** This divides your total budget into three categories and divides your income between them. With this rule, 50% goes towards your NEEDS, 30% goes towards your WANTS, and 20% goes towards your SAVINGS.

- **Zero-Budgeting Approach:** The principle here is that there is a plan for every unit of money you earn. You start with your total income and then plan for bills, expenses, and savings, adjusting your budget until you have nothing left over.

- **Pay Yourself First Approach:** This is all about prioritizing saving for the future. You put a certain percentage of your income into your savings every month and work with whatever's left after that.

You can create a budget yourself on paper or in a spreadsheet, or you could use a budgeting app like Goodbudget. Whichever method you prefer, follow these steps:

- **Note your income.** Note the money you receive from all sources every month.

- **Log your expenses.** Divide your expenses into two categories—fixed (meaning they come out every month and are your NEEDS if you're following the 50/30/20 rule) and discretionary spending. (Discretionary expenses are WANTS and things you spend money on that may change month to month, such as dinner with friends or movie theater tickets.)

- **Plan your savings.** Note the amount of money you can afford to save each month after your expenses have come out.

Once you have a clear idea of how much money you have coming in, how much you're spending, and how much you're saving, you can make adjustments and cut back on expenses as necessary.

A BRIEF GUIDE TO INVESTING

Again, whole books could be written on investing, and we only need to touch the surface here. When you have a lot of savings, you may want to begin investing, and that means deciding what to invest in and being aware of the risks that come with it.

If your eyes glaze over at the mention of the words "stock market," don't worry—you're not alone. It makes my heart palpitate too! It's simply a collection of markets where people buy and sell their shares of companies or corporations. What?! You can buy a share of a company? Yep, you can—that's called an investment. To do this, you'd need to use a stockbroker, who would handle the transaction for you. What you choose to invest in will depend on how much money you can afford to invest and how much you're willing to risk it. Remember, if the company you're investing in goes under, so does your money. Here are your options in a nutshell:

- **Stocks:** These represent partial ownership of a company, and if you have them, you're entitled to a portion of their earnings. They can rise and fall in value on a daily basis, and this makes them a high- risk investment.

- **ETFs (Exchange-Traded Funds):** These are like pies containing a variety of different stocks. When you buy a slice, you're investing in several stocks at the same time. Investing in these is generally less risky than investing in individual stocks because if one company falls in value, the others may rise or at least stay steady.

- **Mutual Funds:** These operate similarly to ETFs in that they contain several different stocks. The difference is that exchange happens only at the end of the day, so trade prices don't vary as much. These are also considered less risky than stocks.

- **Bonds:** These are issued to finance projects and can come from companies, states, cities, or governments. When you buy one, you're essentially lending your money to the issuer, who promises to pay you back with interest. Bond prices are directly related to interest rates, and if rates are high, bond prices will fall.

The Secret to Saving

You've probably been encouraged to save up for things you want ever since you were little, but saving up isn't just for kids. It will serve you your whole life, and it's a good idea to do it as much as possible. The trick is to spend less money than you earn. Your budget will help you with that.

If you like to gamify things, you can make saving fun by setting yourself short, mid, and long-term savings goals. Short-term goals might be things like nice clothes or concert tickets—things you can't necessarily afford to take straight out of your paycheck but which won't take long to save for. Mid-term goals might be things like a vacation, a car, or a new laptop—things that cost a bit more and will take a little longer to save up for. Long-term goals are for the big expenses, often well into the future—things like saving for a house or for your retirement.

How long it takes you to save for your mid and short-term goals will depend on how much you can save each month. If you budget well, you can figure it out and get an idea of how long it will take you. We'll use US dollars in our example, but the same principles apply to whatever currency is used in your country of residence. Imagine you want to save $300 for a new gadget, and your budget will allow you to save $20 a week. You'll meet your goal and get that gadget in 15 weeks. Knowing that from the outset is a great motivator. Sometimes, though, you'll have to work the other way around and start with time. If, for example, you want to save for a concert ticket that's $120, you're limited to the amount of time there is before the tickets go on sale. If you have only four weeks to save before the tickets are released, you'll need to save $30 a week in order to afford them in time.

THE LOWDOWN ON LOANS

A loan is an amount of money you can borrow from an organization and pay back over a period of time. You can get loans to pay for pretty much anything, but some loans are designed for specific things—for example, car loans or mortgages. There are two main types of loans: secured and unsecured. A secured loan is attached to something you own. Mortgages are the best example of this. The lender can repossess your property if you don't pay back what you owe them. Unsecured loans aren't attached to anything you own, but debt collectors can still possess your property if you don't pay back what you've borrowed. This type of loan is usually for a smaller amount than a secured loan and takes less time to pay back. No matter which type they are, loans always accrue interest, which means you'll have to pay back more than you borrowed. To get one, you have to apply to a lender, either online or in person. If they approve your application, the money will be transferred into your account, and you'll pay it back in monthly installments until it's paid off. Just as with credit cards, there are fees for missing payments, and you'll gather extra interest too.

The interest rates on loans are usually fixed, which makes payments easy to budget for, and they're good when you need to borrow money in the long term. You get to decide how long you want to have to pay the loan back, but strangely enough, many lenders will charge fees if you want to pay it back early, and the repayments are often not very flexible. In order to qualify for the best rates, you'll need a good credit score, and unfortunately, the first type of loan you're likely to encounter (the dreaded student loan) will probably come before you've had time to build up your credit score.

A FINAL WORD

Money is a complex topic, and it's best approached with caution. Bear in mind that financial institutions are out to make money, and just because they claim to be helping you, it doesn't mean they are. Watch out for get-rich-quick schemes, which often ask you to give them money before there's any hope of making any. Pay attention to interest rates and repayment terms when it comes to borrowing, and make sure you really are in a position to pay back what you owe before making a commitment. Lastly, never give anyone else access to your bank account—this is for you alone, and you should protect it carefully. It's all very well knowing how to manage your money ... but how are you going to make it? In the next chapter, we'll be looking at education and employment so you can answer that question with confidence. First, though, it's time for our affirmation:

The more I learn about money, the more I make.

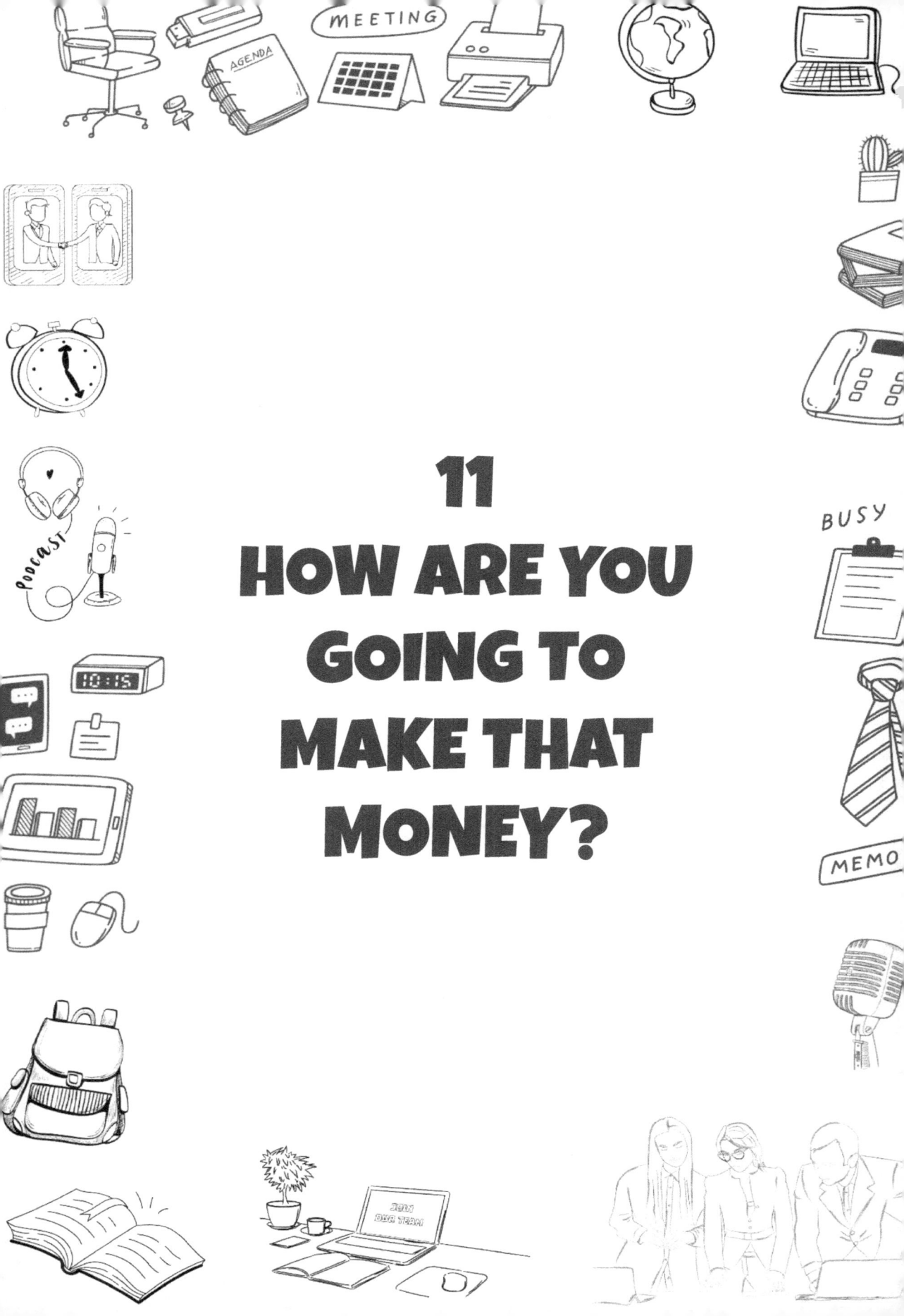

11
HOW ARE YOU GOING TO MAKE THAT MONEY?

My younger cousin recently left for college, and you might be in that position soon too. He's doing a course he's truly interested in, but he didn't choose it without thinking about how useful it would be for his career. He has a solid plan in place for what he wants to do, but it's ok if you don't yet. This chapter is designed to help you think about it. It's ok if you change your mind later, too— many adults (including me!) go through several career changes, and all of it is an important experience. In this chapter, we're going to scratch the surface of higher education and careers. You don't have to figure it all out straight away, but this will give you a starting point to work from.

DO YOU HAVE TO GO TO COLLEGE?

The short answer is no. You have to do what's right for you, and that may be going to college, but it may be that another path is better for you. Here are a few reasons you might want to:

- You know what you want your career to be, and it requires a degree or a set of skills that you'll only be able to learn in college. For example, if you want to be a teacher, you'll need a bachelor's degree in order to qualify for teacher training.

- You like learning, and the idea of academic life appeals to you. In this case, you'll probably find the college experience to be rewarding, and you'll get the chance to meet other people who think as you do.

- You'll be able to take classes that align with your interests while you figure out the direction you eventually want to take.

- You're not sure which of your interests to follow. In this case, you can usually pick your classes so that you can explore different interests before deciding on your major.

- You like the idea of college traditions. If you like the idea of living in dorms with other students or attending college football games, college is your chance to try this lifestyle. It may be hard to justify the expense for this reason alone, but remember you'll also have a degree at the end of it, and you'll probably meet lifelong friends along the way.

- You want to meet people who can get you in the door of your chosen career. Networking is important for many jobs, and college offers you a chance to get your name out to professional organizations you're interested in working with.

If you're still not sure if college is right for you, take a look at the flip side. Here are five reasons why it might not be right for you:

- The job you want to do doesn't require a degree. Training for some jobs happens on the job or through apprenticeships or vocational schools. Sometimes, having a degree will give you the upper hand over other candidates, but weigh out how many more opportunities you'd have—it may be better for you to go straight into training.

- You don't like academic life. School isn't for everyone, and if you hate the environment, the idea of four more years might not appeal. Look into careers that don't require you to have a degree, and see if any of these are a better fit for you.

- Your grades aren't high enough. If you really want to go to college, you may be able to turn your grades around by putting the work in, but it's possible that you won't be accepted if they're not high enough.

- You would only be going because your parents want you to. If you're not sure whether college is for you or you're only doing it to please someone else, consider taking a gap year to allow time to think about it.

- You're concerned about student loan debt. You can fund your education with loans, grants, savings, or scholarships, but debt is a big concern for many people, and it often takes a long time to pay it off. There are a few ways you can mitigate the damage, such as by attending community college in the first year or selecting a state university rather than a private one.

If you think that college may not be right for you, there are a few alternatives you can consider:

- **Community College:** These provide a range of courses that could be transferred to a college, be put towards an associate's degree, or give you access to vocational training. You'll also learn a ton of transferable skills. The admissions process isn't usually very competitive, and you'll generally be able to get into one with lower grades. It'll be cheaper too.

- **Trade School:** For some careers, such as dental assistance or massage therapy, this is a better option than a college degree. The time commitment is often shorter, and the fees are usually lower. Many programs will give you enough skills to qualify within a year.

- **Gap Year:** This is a great option if you're still undecided about college. It's a good opportunity to travel, save for college, or do some volunteer work to get more of an idea of what you might want to do in the future.

- **Apprenticeships:** Apprenticeship programs provide a combination of on-the-job training and classroom instruction. They offer you the chance to receive paid employment while learning a trade or skill from seasoned experts. Apprenticeships are offered in many fields, including manufacturing, healthcare, and construction.

- **Online Courses and Certifications:** You can look into various online classes and certifications that improve your knowledge and abilities in particular fields of interest. Platforms like Coursera, Udemy, and LinkedIn Learning offer a vast selection of online courses taught by industry professionals.

- **Entrepreneurship:** If you have a unique idea or a strong entrepreneurial spirit, consider starting your own business. This path requires self-motivation, determination, and willingness to take risks, but it can offer flexibility and the opportunity to pursue your passion.

THINKING ABOUT YOUR CAREER

Whether you go to college or not, you'll eventually be embarking on a career. If you've been advised to look at career guidance websites, you may well feel overwhelmed by all the options, unsure what your next move should be. My advice is to work backward: instead of focusing on the next move, think about what you want and work backward. Try listing all the companies you'd be excited to work for—set your sights high. Nothing's off the table. Once you have a shortlist, research the companies you've highlighted, and see what they offer. You may find that they offer apprenticeships or grad programs. Look at their vacancies, and see what qualifications you would need if you wanted to apply for one.

You'll probably find that everyone under the sun wants to give you advice about what you should do. Some of it will be good advice; some of it won't. Keep your mind open, and question everything. Bear in mind that any information you read on company websites will be biased. They're not going to tell you about the downsides of working for them; they're going to focus on the good stuff. Talk to as many people as you can, and try to get a balance of information. It may be a good idea to talk to a career counselor, too—they work with young people every day and may be able to help you narrow your focus.

Rather than focusing on the broad picture of your career, think about the skills you can acquire along the way and what work you can do to acquire them. Focus on developing skills like public speaking, networking, project management, and problem-solving, and you'll give yourself a head start on those who haven't yet developed those skills. The world is changing all the time, and the jobs available in 20 years' time may look very different. By focusing on skills rather than roles, you'll put yourself in a better position to secure jobs that don't even exist yet.

You can also use the contacts you have to help you get work experience. If, for example, you're interested in being a solicitor and your mom's friend works at a law firm, it may be possible for you to go in for a couple of weeks and get an idea of the environment. This can be a great way to weed out careers you thought you wanted but don't appeal to you when you actually try them out. Talk to people doing the roles you're interested in and find out what they're really like. Sometimes, the reality can be very different from what we imagine. If only I could rewind time and make a different choice, I might have pursued an alternative path to the one I started out on.

Use your school breaks to try as many different jobs as you can. Summer jobs give you great work experience, increasing your social skills and confidence while bolstering your resume. When you later come to apply for other jobs, you'll be able to reference the skills you've picked up, which could make you a more appealing candidate than your peers. You may enjoy working in a shop one summer, but next summer, try something else—bar work, for example. This way, you get a range of experiences and uplevel your skills in multiple areas. You'll also get a better idea of the kind of work you like, and this will help you zone in on a career path.

My last tip is to get to know yourself. You're working on this all the time, but you can get an even better understanding by doing a personality test. There are plenty available online, and doing one will help you to learn about your strengths and weaknesses. Buzz Quiz is a good one to try.

WRITING A RESUME

Nearly every job you apply for will want to see your resume, and that means you need to know how to write one. Your resume should be tailored for every role you apply for, which means you'll need to tweak it for each application. However, there are some things that you'll need to do every time. Follow this formula, and you'll have the foundation for a killer resume.

Read the job description carefully. Highlight the most important words, and try to include these in your resume while staying honest about the skills and qualifications you have.

Include your contact information. Any potential employers will need this in order to invite you to an interview. Make sure you include your address, phone number, and email address.

Write an objective summary. This will tell the employer what your goals and career ambitions are. It only needs to be a few sentences long—the idea is to grab their attention and give them a clear picture of you. Here's an example: "Diligent high school student with excellent organizational skills. Seeks to expand on customer service skills." Look at this statement every time you apply for a different position. The chances are, you'll want to change it for each one.

Include only information that's relevant to the role. People often think their resume has to include everything, but it's better to focus on the skills and experiences that are relevant to the role. These are the areas you'll need to include:

- **Employment History:** Write down all the jobs you've had in reverse chronological order, describing the main duties and responsibilities.

- **Education:** Write down the name of your school, your grade or the year you graduated, and your grades for different subjects.

- **Skills:** Write down all the skills you have that are relevant to the position you're applying for.

- **Achievements and Awards:** List any relevant awards and achievements you've had in school.

- **Hobbies and Interests:** Omit this section unless your hobbies demonstrate skills that are relevant to the job you're applying for.

Edit and proofread it carefully. Check for errors in spelling and grammar, and make sure your resume reads smoothly. I'd recommend reading it out loud—you'll be amazed by the errors you can catch when you do this. Ideally, you want to get someone else to read it too. A fresh pair of eyes can spot things you'll miss, no matter how many times you read it.

Resume Template - use this simple template to help you with your Resume.

Contact Details

Name

Address

Phone number

Email

Objective Summary

Fill in your experience, your goals, and what makes you the best person for the job.

Experience

List all of your work experience, including the following information:

Job title

Name of company

Dates you were employed between

Bullet points listing your duties and responsibilities

Education

Name of school

Dates attending (including whether you're still in school)

Courses you've completed (with grades)

Skills

List all of your relevant skills in bullet point form.

Achievements and Awards

List all the relevant achievements and awards you've received.

Hobbies and Interests

List any relevant hobbies or interests you have, including the details of any voluntary work you've done.

ACING INTERVIEWS

A good resume will catch an employer's attention, and that may well mean you're invited to an interview. This can be scary, no matter how old you are or how much experience you have (they still scare me now!), but there are a few things you can do to avoid turning into Adam Sandler interviewing for finance positions in The Wedding Singer.

First, research the company, both through its website and through recent news stories and events. Find out about their history and values. This is information you can draw on throughout the interview to show that you've done your due diligence and that you would have the company's interests at heart if you got the role. Find out information about the role as well as the company. This will not only help you answer questions well; it will help you know if it's really the job you want.

Then, read the job description again. Take time to really think about what each duty and responsibility will entail. This will help you know whether you're the right fit for the job, and it will help you to prove it in your interview. For each requirement, make a note of how you meet it, and for every duty, think of a time you've done something similar and note that down too. This will help you prepare for questions you're likely to be asked.

Prepare for interview questions. These will vary depending on the role, but the employer will want to see that you're respectful, responsible, and can meet all of the requirements. Try to communicate your skills and values with every answer you give. It's impossible to predict every question you may be asked, but here are some common ones it's a good idea to prepare for:

- *"Tell me a bit about yourself."* This is your opportunity to show everything you think they should know.

Focus on your experience, skills, and the reason you want to work for the company. You might include the following information in your answer:

1. any relevant work experience

2. relevant interests, awards and achievements at school

3. responsibilities you have at school

4. your career goals

5. personal qualities that will help you in the role

6. your enthusiasm for the job and the company

- *"Tell me about your strengths and weaknesses."* This can be a tough one, so preparing your answer in advance will be helpful. Consider your best qualities, thinking about what other people have said about you. Perhaps you're organized or have excellent time management skills; perhaps you're good with people. Pick the qualities that are most relevant to the role, and focus on those. For your weaknesses, be honest, but be careful not to focus on anything that might give the impression you wouldn't be good at the job. For example, it probably isn't a good idea to tell your employer that you're a perfectionist, but you can tell them that you sometimes get caught up in small details.

- *"What's your availability?"* This is your chance to prove that you're reliable and can work when they need you to. Come prepared with your available hours, bearing in mind that if you're still at school, there may be limitations on how much you're allowed to work. Be careful not to overcommit by promising to work whenever you're needed—be specific about the number of hours you can work and any particular days you'll be unavailable.

- *"Do you have any questions?"* This question throws a lot of people, but it's a great chance to show what you value and demonstrate that you're taking the role seriously. You might ask what the employer would like to see in an employee or what a typical workday would look like. It's ok to ask about pay, but don't make this your only question. Use the opportunity to find out more about the role and demonstrate your interest.

PRO TIP: *Ask a reverse question—for example, "What factors might indicate that I'm not a suitable candidate for this role?" This kind of question puts your employer in a situation where they can't simply refuse you without having a solid argument to back up their decision, especially if you know you're the best candidate for the role.*

- *"Tell me about a time when…"* This question could take a number of turns. They may want to know about times you've navigated a disagreement, made a mistake, or overcome a challenge. They might want to know if you've ever had to take the lead unexpectedly or witnessed something you didn't think was right. Your employer is trying to figure out how you'll react in different situations. You can prepare for this by coming up with a list of anecdotes you can share, focusing on your positive traits.

Your next step is to practice. You may not be able to predict every question, but you can still do a practice run with a friend or one of your parents. It might feel a bit weird, but it will help ease your nerves and give you a chance to practice all your answers.

Don't forget to dress to impress. This will depend on the role you're applying for. In an office environment, a suit or a smart blouse with dress pants would be appropriate; in a restaurant, a smart-casual look might be better. If you're applying for a job in a creative field, let your clothing express your personality while still being smart and professional. Avoid revealing clothes and t-shirts with slogans, and don't wear jeans or sneakers.

Expect to be nervous. Anticipate your usual nervous reactions ahead of time so you manage them as they arise. I know I talk quickly when I'm nervous, for example, so if I'm in a situation where that's likely to happen, I remind myself to slow down and breathe. Acknowledging your nervousness can help you let go of it. Try telling yourself that you can do a good job in this interview, even if your body is nervous. It's amazing how powerful that can be. Why do you think I'm giving you affirmations at the end of every chapter?

Finally, follow up. You don't want to overdo this part, but it shows that you're serious and respectful if you write a thank you email or follow up with a phone call the next day. You can just say that you're grateful for their time and let them know that you'll be happy to provide any extra information they might need. If you don't get the job, you can ask for feedback to help you. Don't be discouraged by their answer—use it to help you improve for the next one.

Now we come to the last and most important skill: staying safe—because none of the rest of the skills you've been learning will matter at all if you're not there to use them. First though, here's your affirmation for this chapter:

I'm deeply valued and generously compensated, regardless of what I do.

12
THE MOST IMPORTANT SKILL OF ALL: STAYING SAFE

Every skill we've looked at is crucial to a seamless transition into adulthood. But none of that will matter unless you know how to look after yourself. So we're ending our journey with the most important skill of all—keeping yourself safe.

EVERYDAY SAFETY TIPS

Make sure there's always someone who knows where you are. If you go out, let your parents know you got there safely, and when you get home, do the same thing for the people you were with.

Remember that you don't have to engage with everyone who approaches you. Be cautious of strangers, no matter what they ask you for. If you feel threatened, attract someone else's attention— that alone will probably be enough to deter the person bothering you.

Don't wear your AirPods or bury yourself in your phone if you're walking alone in the dark. If you're distracted, you're an easy target for criminals.

Don't assume you're safe just because you know the area well. Bad things can happen everywhere, and it's just as important to be vigilant in your local neighborhood as it is in a new area.

Be discrete—keep your valuables out of sight.

PERSONAL SAFETY WHILE YOU' RE WALKING

Wear comfortable shoes that will allow you to get away quickly if you need to.

Be aware of your surroundings at all times. Walk confidently and purposefully, making eye contact with people you pass.

Stay in public areas, avoiding shortcuts through alleys, parks, and fields.

Face oncoming traffic as you walk.

If you feel like someone's following you, don't go home—head for a public place or to a friend's house. You don't want this person to know where you live.

PERSONAL SAFETY ON PUBLIC TRANSPORT

- Plan your route before you set out so you know exactly where you're going and how you're going to get there.

- Check when the last train/bus is, and know how you're going to get home.

- Wait for your transport in a well-lit area, preferably around other people.

- Make sure your ticket or pass is ready so that you can keep your wallet out of sight.

- Avoid empty train cars, especially at night. Try to sit where there are other people around.

- If you don't feel safe or confident, arrange for someone to meet you at the station or bus stop. Report any incidents you witness to the relevant security team.

- If you're using a taxi, make sure it's licensed and ask to see the driver's badge.

- Try to pre-book your ride rather than relying on private-hire vehicles.

- Let someone know the details of the car you're in and where you're going.

- Sit behind the driver so that you're inaccessible.

PERSONAL SAFETY AT HOME

- Be aware of all the windows and doors you have open, and always lock them when you go out.

- When you have your own place, install motion- sensor lights to deter intruders.

- Don't leave your keys by the door or anywhere visible from the outside.

- Don't put your name and address on your keychain. If someone comes to the door claiming to be from a particular organization, ask to see their ID. If it seems suspicious, call the organization to check that the person is who they say they are.

- If you think there's someone inside your home, call the police, and don't enter.

PERSONAL SAFETY IF YOU' RE ALONE AT WORK

on someone else's premises

- Make sure your colleagues know where you are and when you expect to be back.

- Familiarize yourself with the environment, and make sure your phone reception is good.

- Plan an exit strategy just in case.

- Park as close to the location as you can.

- Only carry what you need—too much equipment may make you vulnerable and will make it more difficult to get away easily.

- Wear comfortable clothing that you can move freely in (unless you're restricted by a uniform).

- Make sure you have a clear path to the door.

- Pay attention to your surroundings, and be aware of the exits and any dangers (e.g., dogs).

on Your Work Premises

- Use the intercom system to make sure you know if anyone else is entering the building.

- If you have to handle cash, try to do this out of sight and away from the door.

- Make sure you have access to a working phone and, if possible, a lockable room you can retreat to if necessary.

- Make sure you know where all the emergency exits and escape routes are.

AT Home

- If you have to meet with a client, consider doing this outside the home in a neutral place.

- Let any visitors think there are other people in the house. (You could do this by putting the TV on in another room.)

- Keep your personal items out of any room you invite clients into.

PERSONAL SAFETY WHEN YOU'RE TRAVELING

- Avoid wearing expensive jewelry.

- If you're old enough to drink alcohol, do so responsibly—you're in an unfamiliar place, and you need to have your wits about you.

- Don't carry a large amount of cash. If you do have it with you, carry only what you need, and leave the rest locked in your hotel. Keep your cash card (and credit card if you have one) in a different place to your cash—that way, if something gets stolen, you still have a backup.

- Research common scams in the country you're traveling to before you leave. This will make you less likely to fall for them.

- Find out what the emergency services number is before you travel, and store it in your phone so you can access it quickly.

- Keep your bag close to you at all times, keeping your valuables in discrete, closed pockets.

- Keep a digital copy of your passport. If it's lost or stolen, this will make it easier to get a replacement. Try not to look too obviously like you're a tourist. Dress in the same way the local people do, and don't suddenly stop to take photos.

- Research transportation options in advance so you can make sure you use reputable companies.

- Keep in touch with your family and friends, and make sure someone knows your plans.

- Check with the staff at your hotel if there are any neighborhoods you should avoid, and mark them on your map.

- Make sure you're always aware of your surroundings—again, this isn't a time for your AirPods or to be buried in your phone.

- Trust your instincts. If you don't feel safe, don't waste time analyzing whether you're right or not— focus on removing yourself from the situation instead.

COLLEGE SAFETY TIPS

- Avoid walking around campus alone at night.

- Pour your own drinks at parties, and keep your glass with you at all times so no one can tamper with it.

- If you're drinking alcohol, don't drive. Arrange for an Uber or ask a friend to drive you instead. Don't get into a car with anyone who intends to drive after drinking, no matter how much they try to tell you they're fine to drive.

- Don't study on your own in isolated places after dark.

- Stick with your friends, and don't let anyone go off with a guy or girl you don't know.

- Join the list for campus alerts so that you're informed of any emergency situations quickly.

- Make sure you lock the door to your dorm room or apartment.

ONLINE SAFETY TIPS

- Don't give your personal information out to anyone you meet online.

- Check your privacy settings frequently to make sure your personal information and photographs remain private.

- Think carefully before you post anything—even if you delete it, someone could have taken a screenshot and reposted it before you did.

- Employers often check social media when they're recruiting, so think carefully about what you're comfortable with them seeing and what could get in the way of jobs you might want in the future. Avoid posting anything when you're emotional; give yourself time to make sure you really want to say it.

CRITICAL LIFE SKILLS FOR TEENS

- Choose strong passwords made up of both lowercase and uppercase letters, numbers, and special characters. Don't share your passwords with anyone—no matter how much you trust them.

- Avoid sexting! When you send a compromising photo of yourself, it will never go away, and there's always a risk that it will come back and haunt you later.

- Be aware that public wireless networks aren't secure. If you need to use them, consider using a VPN (virtual private network).

- Avoid clicking on links or downloading files in emails unless you're absolutely sure you can trust them. Malicious links are often how devices get exposed to viruses. Make sure you have good antivirus software on your device too.

- Don't arrange to meet up with anyone you just met online. Not everyone is who they claim to be.

- Order things only from reputable sites. Check if it's running on HTTPS—this shows that it has a security certificate to safeguard your personal information.

- Use social media handles that are different from your name. This way, if you have to sever connections for any reason, no one will be able to find you by email.

- If you receive bullying messages, try your best to ignore them rather than answer them. You can block them to make this easier.

FIRST AID

You don't need to undertake years of first aid training, but it's a good idea to take a basic first aid course if you can. You'll be able to find a course in your local area, but NSC also offers international first-aid training courses, some of which you can complete online. You can visit their website by using this QR code:

There are a few key skills that are generally recommended to learn at any age.

These are:

- CPR

- dealing with seizures

- treating burn

- looking after sprains

- how to administer stitches

- what to do in the event of a concussion or head trauma

- how to handle broken bones

- how to treat shock

- what to do if someone is choking

- dealing with excessive bleeding

If you find a course that covers all of these areas, you know you're onto a winner. If you're not quite ready to go through a first aid course, there are still some important first aid tips you should know as soon as possible. The most basic of these is to know what to do if you need help. If there's a medical emergency in front of you that requires professional assistance, you'll need to call for an ambulance. This means calling:

- 911 if you're in the United States of America, Canada, Mexico, or the Philippines

- 999 if you're in the United Kingdom

- 112 if you're in India or any European country inside the EU

- 000 (also known as Triple Zero) if you're in Australia

- 111 if you're in New Zealand

If you live in another region not covered here, be sure to look up the emergency number if you don't already know it. You'll need to know the address of the location where the emergency has happened so that first responders can find you.

It's important to have first aid provisions at home too, and getting hold of a first aid kit will be important when you first live on your own. You should have essential medical provisions like pain relievers, antibiotic cream, cold medicine, bandages, and gauze, and you should also have a digital thermometer.

Here's a quick guide to treating the injuries and ailments you're most likely to encounter:

MINOR CUTS/SCRAPES AND BURNS

If you have a cut or scrape:

- Apply a clean cloth to the wound.

- Clean the affected area with water and apply antibiotic ointment.

- Cover the area with a bandage, changing it if it gets dirty or wet.

If you have a burn:

- Hold the affected area under cool water for 5 minutes and lightly place a gauze over the top, don't apply ointment or use ice.

- If a blister forms, don't break it.

- Take painkillers if necessary.

- If a cut or burn becomes infected, seek help from a professional.

SPRAINS AND STRAINS

Rest, ice, compression, and elevation (RICE) are the recommended remedies for sprains and strains. Over-the-counter pain medications such as acetaminophen or ibuprofen can also be used to relieve pain and inflammation.

CONCUSSIONS

Rest and monitoring of symptoms are the primary treatments for concussions. It's important to seek medical attention if symptoms such as headache, dizziness, confusion, or vomiting persist.

FRACTURES

Seek medical attention immediately. A doctor will perform an X-ray or other diagnostic tests to confirm the fracture and develop an appropriate treatment plan.

If possible, immobilize the injured area using a splint or brace to prevent further damage. For example, if the fracture is in your arm, use a sling to immobilize the arm.

COLD AND FLU

If your fever is below 101.5°F (38.6°C), you can take the following measures at home to manage it:

- **Rest:** It's important to rest and avoid strenuous activities so that your immune system has all the energy it needs to make you better.

- **Hydration:** Drink plenty of fluids such as water, herbal tea, or clear broths to help prevent dehydration.

- **Medications:** Over-the-counter treatments such as acetaminophen or ibuprofen can be used to reduce fever and relieve discomfort. Always follow the recommended dosage on the label, and avoid exceeding the maximum daily dose.

- **Cool Compresses:** Apply a cool, damp cloth or towel to your forehead or the back of your neck to help lower your body temperature.

- **Clothing:** Wear light and breathable clothing to prevent overheating.

It's important to note that if your fever is persistent, rises above 101.5°F (38.6°C), or is accompanied by other symptoms such as vomiting, diarrhea, or a rash, it's best to seek medical attention.

MENTAL HEALTH ISSUES

Seeking professional help from a therapist or counselor can be effective in treating mental health issues such as anxiety, depression, or stress. Medications may also be prescribed in some cases.

Your safety is the most important thing, and if you can keep yourself safe, you already have everything you need for adulthood: yourself. All the other skills you've learned are important, but remember, you can always keep building on them and picking up more as you go along. In fact, you should, a successful adult never stops learning and growing. And with that in mind, here's your affirmation for this chapter:

Every day, I get better and grow as a person.

PSSST! PASS IT ON

Tell your friends about this book, share the skills you've learned, and infect someone you've never met with the thirst for knowledge!

Simply by sharing your honest opinion of this book on Amazon, you'll show other teenagers where they can find all the guidance they need to step into adulthood with confidence.

Thank you so much for your help. Let's flood a whole generation with the skills they need to be happy and successful adults!

https://geni.us/writeabookreview

CONCLUSION

So there you have it. You have the keys to adulthood in your back pocket, and you have everything it takes to be successful going forward. We've touched on everything from personal relationships to cooking skills, so don't be alarmed if you don't remember everything. This book will be here for you as long as you need it. Go back to the sections you need to, whip it out when you're unsure of what to do about something, and keep repeating those affirmations to yourself. Most importantly, never stop learning and growing. We may all have to grow up eventually, but there's no such thing as being fully grown—there's always more to learn, and that's one of the most beautiful things about life.

I've worked with many young people over the years, and I know that learning the life skills and social skills we've discussed here has served them well. They'll do that for you, too. Start practicing these skills now, before you leave home. Offer to help your parents so you can get some extra practice. The best way to learn is to do, and I'm absolutely certain that they'll be grateful for the help and proud of the person you are.

Share what you've learned with your friends, and better yet, tell them about the book so they can get all the benefits you have, and to take it a step further ... you could help me out by leaving a review on Amazon. That way, even more young people will find it—and your chances of finding roommates who have the same skills you do will increase! No one wants to share a kitchen with the girl who comes home with a whole chicken expecting to whip up a pasta dish with it in five minutes, let me tell you!

And as we wrap up our journey together, I'd like to leave you with one last affirmation. Say these to yourself often, and believe them. You're awesome, and you've got an amazing life ahead of you.

I can be whatever I want to be.

REFERENCES

Abrahams, C. (2021, March 9). *Personal safety tips & advice*. Peoplesafe. https:// peoplesafe.co.uk/blogs/personal-safety-tips-advice/

Acne - Symptoms and causes. (2022, May 25). Mayo Clinic. https://www. mayoclinic.org/diseases-conditions/acne/symptoms-causes/syc-20368047

Are you getting enough sleep? (2022, September 19). cdc.gov. https://www. cdc. gov/sleep/features/getting-enough-sleep.html

Back on Track Teens. (January 20). *How to build effective relationships as a teenager.* Back On Track Teens. https://www.backontrackteens.com/blog/build-effective-relationships-as-teenager/

Bailey, J. (2021, February 28). *Teaching your teen the basics of auto maintenance*. 2 Dads with Baggage. https://2dadswithbaggage.com/teaching-your-teen- the-basics-of-auto-maintenance/

Bariso, J. (2019, September 30). Inc.com. *inc.com*. https://www.inc.com/justin-bariso/28-emotional-intelligence-quotes-that-can-help-make-emotions-work-for-you-instead-of-against-you.html

Basic first aid skills everyone should learn. (2021, January 15). atr-ltd.co.uk. https://atr-ltd.co.uk/news/basic-first-aid-skills-everyone-should-learn/

A beginner's guide to goal setting for teens. (2023, January 2). Powerful Youth. https://powerfulyouth.com/beginners-guide-goal-setting-for-teens- smart-goals/

Bertone, H. J., & Hoshaw, C. (2021, November 5). *Which type of meditation is right for you?* Healthline. https://www.healthline.com/health/mental-health/types-of-meditation

Borison, R. (2014, June 30). *First aid 101 for teens - Your teen mag*. Your Teen Magazine. https://yourteenmag.com/health/physical-health/move-skills- first-aid

Bourne, L. (2014, January 22). *How to do everything better: 8 knife skills everyone should master.* StyleCaster. https://stylecaster.com/8-knife-skills-master/

Career advice tips for teens; 13 practical tips to help you figure it all out. (2021, November 14). 1000 Years of Career Advice. https://www.1000year-sofca reeradvice.com/career-advice-tips-for-teens/

Celes. (2022, July 3). *8 tips to be empathetic to others.* Personal Excellence. https://personalexcellence.co/blog/empathy/

Characteristics of healthy & unhealthy relationships. (n.d.). Youth.gov. https://youth.gov/youth-topics/teen-dating-violence/characteristics

Chen, J. (2022, July 21). *Exchange rates: What they are, how they work, why they fluctuate.* Investopedia. https://www.investopedia.com/terms/e/ ex-changerate.asp

Cherry K. (2022, December 1). *The 6 types of basic emotions and their effect on human behavior.* Verywell Mind. https://www.verywellmind.com/an-over view-of-the-types-of-emotions-4163976

Cherry, K. (2023, February 23). *Understanding body language and facial expressions.* Verywell Mind. https://www.verywellmind.com/under-stand-body- language-and-facial-expressions-4147228

Clayton, L. (2022, July 18). *How to clean a living room—an expert guide.* homesandgardens.com. https://www.homesandgardens.com/interior-de-sign/ living-rooms/how-to-clean-a-living-room

Cookist. (2018, April 3). *12 cooking skills every young adult should learn.* Cookist.com. https://www.cookist.com/12-cooking-skills-every-young-adult-should-learn/

Cottingham, D. (2019, February 5). *Learning to navigate. Highway Code Re-sources.* https://mocktheorytest.com/resources/learning-to-navigate/

Covey, S. R. (2013). *The / habits of highly effective people: Powerful lessons in personal change.* Simon & Schuster.

Cowen, A. S., & Keltner, D. (2017, September 5). *Just a moment ...* https://www. pnas.org/doi/full/10.1073/pnas.1702247114

Crevin, M. (2021, January 14). *Listen more, talk less and other tips for better communication - Your teen mag.* Your Teen Magazine. https://yourteenmag. com/family-life/communication/ways-to-improve-communication

Crevin, M. (2022, August 9). *8 tips to help your teen communicate more effectively in today's digital world.* parentingteensandtweens.com. https://parenting teensandtweens.com/eight-communication-skills-for-teens/

Davidson, S. (2022, August 25). *Five things all teenagers need to know about money.* Metro. https://metro.co.uk/2022/08/25/five-things-all-teenagers-need-to-know-about-money-17241318/

Dietary reference intakes for energy, carbohydrate, fiber, fat, fatty acids, cholesterol, protein and amino acids. (2002). The National Academies Press.

Different Types of Relationships. (n.d.). Assert supports autistic adults in Brighton and Hove - Assert Brighton and Hove. https://assertbh.org.uk/ wp-content/uploads/2016/08/Different-Types-of-Relationships.pdf

Driving in a foreign country. (n.d.). Wikitravel - The Free Travel Guide. Retrieved April 24, 2023, from https://wikitravel.org/en/ Driving_in_a_foreign_country

Eat This, Not That!. (2021, February 23). *Secret hacks to pick the perfect produce every time.* https://www.eatthis.com/produce-shopping-tips/

Edberg, H. (2022, January 20). *17 inspirational quotes on people skills.* The Positivity Blog. https://www.positivityblog.com/17-inspirational-quotes-on-people-skills/

8 important car maintenance services teens and new drivers need to know. (n.d.). Business and Personal Insurance Solutions | Travelers Insurance. https:// www.travelers.com/resources/auto/maintenance/8-important-car-main tenance-services-teens-need-to-know

Eisenhower's urgent/important principle. (n.d.). Develop your personal well-being and career skills - Mind Tools - Mind Tools. https://www.mindtools. com/ al1e0k5/eisenhowers-urgentimportant-principle

Elkus, G. (2022, July 21). *The ultimate guide to picking only the best produce.* Real Simple. https://www.realsimple.com/food-recipes/shopping-storing/ how-to-pick-produce

Emergency numbers list: 911, 112 & 999 numbers worldwide. (n.d.). Adducation. https://www.adducation.info/general-knowledge-travel-and-transport/ emergency-numbers/

Era, Y. (2021, March 26). *How to use skills to logically solve a problem.* Youth Empowerment. https://youthempowerment.com/problem-solving/

Felman, A. (2023, April 19). *What is health?: Defining and preserving good health.* Medical and health information. https:// www.medicalnewstoday.com/ articles/150999#what_is_health

Four steps to identifying emotions — Reflection counselling services. (2017, September 7). Reflection Counselling Services. https://www.reflection counselling.ca/blog/2017/9/4/how-to-identify-your-feelings

Frost, A. (2021, September 9). *9 job interview tips for teens.* The Muse. https:// www.themuse.com/advice/job-interview-tips-for-teens

Garrity, A. (2020, March 12). *A cleaning expert explains how to clean your bathroom from top to bottom.* Good Housekeeping. https:// www.goodhouse-keep ing.com/home/cleaning/g31292850/how-to-clean-bathroom/

GoHenry. (2023, January 9). *Budgeting for teens: A guide for parents and teenagers.* https://www.gohenry.com/uk/blog/financial-education/how- to-teach-your-teenager-about-budgeting

Gongala, S. (2023, February 13). *21 essential life skills for teens to learn.* MomJunction. https://www.momjunction.com/articles/everyday-life-skills-your-teen-should-learn_0081859/

The Good Housekeeping Cookery Team. (2014, October 20). *How to choose lamb.* Good Housekeeping. https://www.goodhousekeeping.com/uk/ food/ cookery-videos/a657324/how-to-choose-lamb/

A guide for choosing the right type of meat for your meal. (n.d.). Fresh Farms. https://www.freshfarms.com/a-guide-to-choosing-the-right-type-of- meat-for-your-meal/

H, J. (2021, January 30). *How to teach teens that how they dress matters.* Mommy Bunch. https://mommybunch.com/teach-teens-appropriate-dress-with out-lecturing/

Hauck, C. (2018, October 11). *A 10-minute meditation to work with difficult emotions.* Mindful. https://www.mindful.org/a-10-minute-meditation-to-work-with-difficult-emotions/

Herrity, J. (2022, November 4). *Should you go to college? 5 reasons you should (or shouldn't).* Indeed Career Guide. https://www.indeed.com/career-advice/ career-development/should-i-go-to-college

Hill, G. (2021, August 1). *45 cooking affirmations to make better food.* MagicAffirmations.org | Passionate having a positive vibe. https://magicaffirmations. org/cooking-affirmations/

Holdefehr, K. (2022, August 6). *9 basic home maintenance how-tos everyone should know.* Real Simple. https://www.realsimple.com/home-organizing/ home-improvement/maintenance-repairs/home-maintenance-basics

How much physical activity do you need? (2021, July 19). Centers for Disease Control and Prevention. https://www.cdc.gov/physicalactivity/basics/age-chart.html

How to cook perfect rice. (2014, December 8). Great British Chefs. https://www. greatbritishchefs.com/how-to-cook/how-to-cook-rice

How to move out of your parents' house. (2021, August 2). safestore. https://www. safestore.co.uk/blog/2021/08/how-to-move-out-of-your-parents-house/

The importance of good manners. (n.d.). Headspace. https://www.headspace. com/articles/the-importance-of-good-manners

Indeed Editorial Team. (2023, February 25). *How to write a resume for a teenager: top tips.* Indeed. https://au.indeed.com/career-advice/resumes-cover-letters/how-to-write-resume-for-teenager

International first aid training. (n.d.). National Safety Council - Save lives, from the workplace to anyplace. https://www.nsc.org/safety-training/inter-national/international-first-aid-training

Kass, J. (2017, March 28). *Car maintenance 101 for teen drivers.* Drive Smart Georgia. https://drivesmartgeorgia.com/blog/car-maintenance-101-teen- drivers/

Keech, D. (2022, October 31). *15 home maintenance tasks and repairs everyone should know how to do.* MilitaryByOwner Housing Blog. https://blog.mili tarybyowner.com/15-home-maintenance-tasks-and-repairs-everyone- should-know-how-to-do

Khona, M. (2022, August 25). *16 effective skin care tips for teenagers.* SkinKraft. https://skinkraft.com/blogs/articles/skin-care-tips-for-teenagers

Kimberli. (2023, April 2). *15 simple travel safety tips everyone should know.* Worldpackers: Work Exchange, Volunteer Abroad, Gap Year. https:// www. worldpackers.com/articles/simple-travel-safety-tips

Krockow, E. (2018, September 27). *How many decisions do we make each day?* Psychology Today. https://www.psychologytoday.com/gb/blog/stretch ing-theory/201809/how-many-decisions-do-we-make-each-day

Kubala, J. (2022, June 20). *Healthy eating for teens: What you need to know.* Healthline. https://www.healthline.com/nutrition/healthy-eating-for-teens

Lane, M. (2021, October 27). *A beginner's guide to loans | money.co.uk.* Take control of your money — Compare credit cards, loans, mortgages & more. https://www.money.co.uk/loans/a-beginners-guide-to-loans

Larsen, L. (2021, April 8). *How to read a cooking recipe for simple spaghetti.* The Spruce Eats. https://www.thespruceeats.com/how-to-read-a-cooking- recipe-481265

Lee, R. (2022, March 19). *The top 8 most tradable currencies.* Investopedia. https://www.investopedia.com/trading/most-tradable-currencies/

Leigh, M. P. (2017, November 15). *The importance of the decision making process.* EverydayHealth.com. https://www.everydayhealth.com/neurology/impor tance-decision-making-process/

Lienard, S. (2014, September 22). *25 skills every cook should know.* BBC Good Food | Recipes and cooking tips - BBC Good Food. https://www.bbc-good food.com/howto/guide/25-skills-every-cook-should-know

Loop, E. (2013, June 18). *How to adult.* How To Adult. https://howtoadult. com/reasons-teens-should-drive-6174.html

MacKay, J. (2019, December 16). *50 inspirational (and actionable) time management quotes - RescueTime.* RescueTime Blog. https://blog.rescuetime.com/ time-management-quotes/

Make a healthy grocery list in minutes. (2022, November 26). WebMD. https:// www.webmd.com/food-recipes/guide/grocery-list

Marlin, D. (2017, April 21). 27 *quotes to change how you think about problems.* Entrepreneur. https://www.entrepreneur.com/leadership/27-quotes-to- change-how-you-think-about-problems/288957

Mattson, A. (2021, February 24). *Health tips for teens every young person needs to learn.* Harmony Healthcare Long Island. https://www.harmony-health careli.org/health-tips-for-teens/

Menstrual hygiene. (2022, December 1). Centers for Disease Control and Prevention.   https://www.cdc.gov/hygiene/personal-hygiene/ menstrual. html

Meurisse, T. (2018). Upgrade yourself: *Simple strategies to transform your mindset, improve your mindset, improve your habits and change your life.*

Middleearthnj. (2019, September 30). *Teaching teens what a healthy relationship looks like.* Middle Earth. https://middleearthnj.org/2019/09/30/ teaching- teens-what-a-healthy-relationship-looks-like/

Minimum driving age by country - Rhinocarhire.com. (n.d.). Car Hire - Cheap Car Rental Worldwide from Rhinocarhire.com. https://www.rhinocarhire. com/Drive-Smart-Blog/Minimum-Driving-Age-Country.aspx

Money affirmations. Do they really work? (n.d.). Saving in London City. https:// savinginlondoncity.com/blog/money-affirmations/

Morin, A. (2021, January 31). *Steps to good decision making skills for teens. Verywell Family.* https://www.verywellfamily.com/steps-to-good-deci sion-making-skills-for-teens-2609104

Morrisey, B. (2021, March 8). *Beauty tips for boys.* What Teenagers Want to Know. https://www.teenissues.co.uk/beautytipsforboys.html

Naylon, J. (2005, March 15). *The easiest way to clean your room.* wikiHow. Retrieved April 24, 2023, from https://www.wikihow.com/Clean-Your-Room

Newton, N. D. (2020, November 25). *Making good decisions: A priceless life skill.* International School Parent. https://www.internationalschoolparent. com/articles/making-good-decisions/

O'Donnell, J. (2021, February 22). *Tips for teaching your tween boy to shave safely.* Verywell Family. https://www.verywellfamily.com/shaving-tips-for-preteen-boys-3288402

Online safety. (2022, August). Nemours KidsHealth - the Web's most visited site about children's health. https://kidshealth.org/en/teens/internet-safe-ty.html

Oral health advice for teenagers. (2019, July). NHS Ayrshire & Arran. https:// www.nhsaaa.net/media/7729/mis11-024-gd-oral-health_teenagers-information-leaflet.pdf

Oral health: A window to your overall health. (2021, October 28). Mayo Clinic. https://www.mayoclinic.org/healthy-lifestyle/adult-health/in-depth/ den-tal/art-20047475

Organising Skills. (n.d.). skillsyouneed. https://www.skillsyouneed.com/ lead/ organising-skills.html

Parents rarely let go of their children, so children let go of them. T ... -Mitch Albom | Mitch Albom quotes. (n.d.). Quotss. https://www.quotss.com/ quote/Parents-rarely-let-go-of-their-children-so-children-let-go-of-them-They-m

Patwal, S. (2023, April 6). *Personal hygiene for teens: Importance and tips to teach them.* MomJunction. https://www.momjunction.com/articles/ hygiene- tips-for-your-teens_00116170/

Pierce, R. (2023, March 14). *13 practical time management skills to teach teens.* Life Skills Advocate. https://lifeskillsadvocate.com/blog/13-practical- time-management-skills-to-teach-teens/

Podl, J. (2019, September 19). *The best - and hardest - Thing we can do to prepare our teens for adulthood - Your teen mag.* Your Teen Magazine. https://yourteenmag. com/health/teenager-mental-health/indepen-dent-living-skills-for-teens

Poncelet, A. B. (2021, October 6). *How to teach your teen good hygiene.* Very-well Family. https://www.verywellfamily.com/smelly-teen-lets-talk-teen- hygiene-3200879

Purles, K. (2022, January 12). *Sweat glands: The science behind sweat.* SweatBlock. https://www.sweatblock.com/sweat-glands/

Quitmeyer, M. (2020, November 8). *41 cooking basics you should probably know by now.* BuzzFeed. https://www.buzzfeed.com/maitlandquitmeyer/cook ing-basics-everyone-should-know

Raypole, C. (2020, April 28). *How to control your emotions: 11 strategies to try.* Healthline. https://www.healthline.com/health/how-to-control-your- emotions

The reason why teens can't get up in the morning. (2017, October 26). Mumbai Mirror. https://mumbaimirror.indiatimes.com/others/health-life-style/ the-reason-why-teens-cant-get-up-in-the-morning/articleshow/ 61229029.cms

Relationship communication skills for teenagers. (n.d.). Planned Parenthood | Official Site. https://www.plannedparenthood.org/learn/teens/relation ships/all-about-communication

Renée. (2018, October 14). *Household management life skills to teach gifted teens.* Great Peace Living. https://reneeatgreatpeace.com/household-man-age ment-life-skills/

Renée. (2018, September 4). *Cooking 101 life skills for gifted teens.* Great Peace Living. https://reneeatgreatpeace.com/cooking-life-skills-gifted-teens/

Reynolds, N. (2022, March 9). *50 potentially life-saving safety tips every teenager should know.* Raising Teens Today. https://raisingteenstoday.com/ safety- tips-every-teenager-should-know/

Rogers, K. (2022, December 14). *Do you really need deodorant? Experts weigh in.* CNN. https://edition.cnn.com/2022/12/13/health/is-deodorant-necessary-antiperspirant-tips-wellness/index.html

Sandeep. (2022, August 15). *85 best growth mindset affirmations for teens | 2023.* Positive Miracle. https://positivemiracle.com/growth-mindset-affir-ma tions-for-teens/

Secrets to picking top quality meat | Markets at Shrewsbury. (2017, August 25). The Markets at Shrewsbury. https://www.marketsatshrewsbury.com/ blog/ secret-picking-top-quality-meat/

7 great reasons why exercise matters. (2021, October 8). Mayo Clinic. https://www.mayoclinic.org/healthy-lifestyle/fitness/in-depth/exercise/ art- 20048389

Shameer, M. (2023, April 6). *Top 25 social skills activities for teens and young children.* MomJunction. https://www.momjunction.com/articles/so-cial-skills- activities-for-teens_00352014/

Sharma, R. (2019). *Five ways to rise above a hard time* [Video]. YouTube. https:// www.youtube.com/watch?v=EZUyv0Iry30&ab_channel=RobinShar-ma

Shaving tips for teen girls. (2022, December 7). WebMD. https://teens. webmd.com/shaving-tips-girls

Silver, C. (2023, March 9). *The ultimate guide to financial literacy. Investope-dia.* https://www.investopedia.com/guide-to-financial-literacy-4800530

Sippl, A. (2023, January 26). *7 organization skills to teach your teen.* Life Skills Advocate. https://lifeskillsadvocate.com/blog/7-organiza-tion-skills-to- teach-your-teen/

Skin care for children and teens. (n.d.). https://www.boystownpediatrics.org/ knowledge-center/skin-care-children-teens

Skin care tips for teens. (2021, September 24). WebMD. https://teens.web-md. com/teen-skin-care-tips

Spoon U. (2016, November 14). *9 grocery store hacks to know before heading to college.* Teen Vogue. https://www.teenvogue.com/story/what-to-know-about-grocery-shopping-in-college

Spots: *Just the facts.* (2020, June 5). Health For Teens. https:// www.healthforteens.co.uk/growing-up/spots/spots-just-the-facts/

St Pierre Ms Rd, B. (2023). Infographic | The Best Calorie Control Guide. *Precision Nutrition.* https://www.precisionnutrition.com/calorie- con-trol-guide-infographic

Stojanovic, M. (2023, March 1). *How to break a project down into tasks.* Clockify Blog. https://clockify.me/blog/productivity/break-project-into-tasks/

Sutton, J. (2020, October 7). *Understanding emotions: 15 ways to identify your feelings.* PositivePsychology.com. https://positivepsychology.com/under standing-emotions/

Take charge of your health: A guide for teenagers. (2016, December 1). National Institute of Diabetes and Digestive and Kidney Diseases. https://www. niddk.nih.gov/health-information/weight-management/take-charge- health-guide-teenagers

Teaching your child healthy nail care. (n.d.). American Academy of Dermatology. https://www.aad.org/public/everyday-care/nail-care-secrets/basics/nail- care

Teen driving 101: A step-by-step test of essential driving skills. (2022, January 17). State Farm. https://www.statefarm.com/simple-insights/au-to-and-vehi cles/teen-driving-101-a-stepbystep-test-of-essential-skills

10 reasons why time management is important. (n.d.). Brainbridge workforce solutions | Brainbridge. https://www.brainbridge.be/en/news/10-reasons-why-time-management-is-important

Thrive Training and Consulting. (2021, November 11). *Tips for teens: Building healthy communication skills.* Thrive Training Consulting. https://www. thrivetrainingconsulting.com/tips-for-teens-building-healthy-communi cation-skills/

Top 10 conflict resolution skills for teens — Personal Excellence Foundation. (2022, December 8). Personal Excellence Foundation. https://perso-nalexcellence. org/raising-worldchangers-blog/top-10-conflict-resolution-skills-for- teens

Top 25 sharing knowledge quotes. (n.d.). A-Z Quotes. https://www. azquotes.com/quotes/topics/sharing-knowledge.html

TruBlu Dentistry. (2019, November 7). *The pros and cons of teeth whitening.* https://www.trubludentistry.com/blog/the-pros-and-cons-of-teeth-whitening/

Ultimate guide: Copper's guide to saving money (for teens). (2023, April 24). Banking, investing and learning for your family. https://www.getcop-per.com/guide/saving

Understanding currencies and exchange rates. (n.d.). World101 from the Council on Foreign Relations. https://world101.cfr.org/global-era-issues/mone tary-policy-and-currencies/understanding-currencies-and-ex-change- rates

Vincent, E. (2021, June 10). *Life skills for teens: How to clean the kitchen (with printable checklists).* Weird, Unsocialized Homeschoolers. https://www. weirdunsocializedhomeschoolers.com/life-skills-for-teens-how-to-clean- the-kitchen/

Vogel, K. (2023, March 21). *Parade.com.* parade.com. https://parade.com/1179956/kaitlin-vogel/health-quotes/

Vora, D. (2022, October 20). *How to establish the right hair care routine for teenagers.* MyCocoSoul. https://mycocosoul.com/blogs/hair-care-regi men/teenage-hair-care-routine

Vyas, D. (2022, April 7). *Guide to developing growth mindset for teens.* LinkedIn. https://www.linkedin.com/pulse/guide-developing-growth-mind-set- teens-deepali-vyas/?trk=articles_directory

Wehrli, A. (2021, January 8). *Basic first aid skills all children should know.* Moms. https://www.moms.com/first-aid-skills-kids/

What are emotions and why do they matter? (2015, March 31). iMotions. https:// imotions.com/blog/learning/research-fundamentals/emo-tions-matter/

What are problem solving skills | Build skills for life and work | Young professional.(2022, August 20). Youth Employment UK. https://www.youthemploy ment.org.uk/young-professional-training/problem-solving-skills-young- professional/

What is time management? (n.d.). Develop your personal wellbeing and career skills - Mind Tools - Mind Tools. https://www.mindtools.com/arb6j5a/what-is-time-management

Where to exchange currency at the cheapest rate. (2022, October 24). Investopedia. https://www.investopedia.com/articles/personal-finance/082114/best- places-exchange-currency.asp

Why is sleep important? (2022, March 24). NHLBI, NIH. https://www.nhlbi.nih.gov/health/sleep/why-sleep-important

Why you should learn to drive—the benefits of driving—The Yale wave. (2022, April 28). Yale University—WordPress for Individuals and Groups @ Yale University. https://campuspress.yale.edu/wave/why-you-should-learn-to-drive-the-benefits-of-driving/

Witmer, D. (2020, May 13). *14 essential manners every teen should know.* Verywell Family. https://www.verywellfamily.com/manners-your-teen-should-use-and-how-to-teach-them-2608864

A GIFT FOR YOU

The ultimate planner for teens
- With goal-setting and time management features
- To improve study habits and personal development
- Goal-oriented with daily, weekly, and monthly layouts
- With journaling prompts for self-reflection and growth
  And much more!

SCAN me